SPONSORS

Capitol | $10,000
American Institute of Architects, Nebraska Chapter
HDR Architecture

Union Station | $5,000
DLR Group
James C. and Rhonda S. Seacrest Foundation

Buffalo Bill House | $2,500
First National Bank
Leo A Daly
RDG Planning & Design

Log Cabin | $1,000
Alley Poyner Macchietto Architecture
American Institute of Architects, Lincoln
American Institute of Architects, Omaha
Studio 951, Inc.
Anonymous Donation

Log Cabin | $500

Individuals
Merle Bachman, AIA
Gary Bowen, FAIA
Bryce Hastings, AIA
Larry Jacobsen, AIA
Sara Kay, Hon AIA & James Walbridge, AIA

Firms & Organizations
American Institute of Architects, Western Nebraska
Berggren Architects
BVH Architecture
CMBA Architects
Davis Design
E & A Consulting
Fireplace Stone & Patio
Nebraska Masonry Alliance
Schemmer Associates
Sinclair Hille
UNL College of Architecture

In-Kind Contribution
Jeff Barnes

150@150

NEBRASKA'S LANDMARK BUILDINGS
at the State's Sesquicentennial

Jeff Barnes

Buffalo Bill Cody's Home in North Platte.

All photographs by Jeff Barnes, unless otherwise credited

COPYRIGHT © 2017 by the Architectural Foundation of Nebraska

All rights reserved, including the right to reproduce this work in any form whatsoever without permission in writing from the publisher, except for brief passages in connection with a review. For information, please write:

The Donning Company Publishers
731 S. Brunswick Street
Brookfield, MO 64628

Lex Cavanah, General Manager
Nathan Stufflebean, Production Supervisor
Heather L. Floyd, Editor
Terry Epps, Graphic Designer
Alyssa Niemeier, Project Research Coordinator
Katie Gardner, Marketing and Project Coordinator

Barry Haire, Project Director

Library of Congress Cataloging-in-Publication Data

Names: Barnes, Jeff, 1958- author.
Title: 150@150 : Nebraska's landmark buildings at the state's
    sesquicentennial / by Jeff Barnes.
Other titles: One hundred fifty at one hundred fifty
Description: Brookfield, MO : The Donning Company Publishers, 2017. |
    Includes bibliographical references and index.
Identifiers: LCCN 2017043531 | ISBN 9781681841496 (hardcover : alk. paper)
Subjects: LCSH: Historic buildings--Nebraska. |
    Architecture--Nebraska--History. | Nebraska--History.
Classification: LCC F667 .B37 2017 | DDC 978.2--dc23
LC record available at https://lccn.loc.gov/2017043531

Printed in the United States of America at Walsworth

Table of Contents

Preface
6

Chapter 1: **The New Territory**
8

Chapter 2: **The New State/1867 to 1879**
14

Chapter 3: **Building the West/The 1880s**
28

Chapter 4: **Wealth to Build/The 1890s**
38

Chapter 5: **The New Century/The 1900s**
48

Thomas Rogers Kimball: A Legacy
60

Chapter 6: **Laying the Track/The 1910s**
62

Chapter 7: **Challenging Conventions/The 1920s**
72

Chapter 8: **Depression, Drought, and Deco/The 1930s**
84

Chapter 9: **War and Post-War/The 1940s**
92

Chapter 10: **Moving Toward Modern/The 1950s**
100

Chapter 11: **Legends on the Landscape/The 1960s**
106

Chapter 12: **Economy and Energy/The 1970s**
112

Chapter 13: **Building Through Recession/The 1980s and 1990s**
118

Chapter 14: **Entering the New Millennium/The 2000s**
128

Chapter 15: **Designing for the Next 150/The 2010s**
140

Bibliography
152

Acknowledgments
156

Index
157

First-Plymouth Congregational Church in Lincoln.

Preface

I was approached in June 2016 by Sara Kay, executive director of The American Institute of Architects of Nebraska, about a gift the foundation wanted to present to the people of Nebraska for the state's 150th birthday—a book featuring a like number of Nebraska's landmark buildings.

The idea was perfect. Nebraska has a rich heritage of landmark structures, with hundreds of sites in the National Register of Historic Places. I had places in mind, places I'd visited before, and I was already mapping out trips to them. The book would practically write itself. However, putting together a book of 150 Nebraska landmark buildings to commemorate the state's 150th birthday was more difficult than one might expect.

So many criteria could be used in how a building could qualify to be featured in the book—its age, its association with a famous Nebraskan or a famous architect, or its representation of a particular style, industry, or region of the state were all valid points.

We soon decided that this book could not be a "best of" collection, as architecture can be a highly subjective art, and while this would be a book from the architectural community, it could not be one about or for that community.

Creating a collection of the "most historic" buildings in Nebraska history wasn't the path, either, as many of those buildings have been torn down, destroyed by fire or storm, or simply decayed. Quite often, the history of a building is not the events or the personalities associated with it, but the lives lived in that church, business, or home or the statement they wanted to make with its construction.

Initially, there was the hope that we could have a building from each of the ninety-three counties, or one from each year of statehood. Following both paths would, of course, have eliminated remarkable structures for purely arbitrary reasons.

Ultimately, it came down to what buildings survived to help tell the story of Nebraska, its people, and the built world they created for themselves. In compiling the entries for the book, the goal was to highlight the rich diversity of the land, the people, and the traditions of Nebraska through its architecture. Our hope was to cover as broad a geographic area, to highlight as many social groups and industries, and to recognize as many citizens who brought fame to the state as possible. Finally, to close the book, we highlighted the architectural gems and wonders built in our own time that impact lives today.

There will naturally be criticism of worthy projects not being included, or of too much emphasis on the major cities (or on just one of the cities). I've followed Nebraska history long enough to know that's been a criticism on nearly every issue since Nebraska became a state!

Nonetheless, I think much of what we do have will please and delight the readers for our Nebraska sesquicentennial year.

Jeff Barnes
Omaha
July 30, 2017

This Bellevue log cabin is possibly the oldest building in Nebraska. Local legend has its construction from circa 1835.

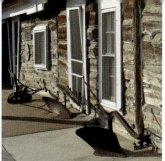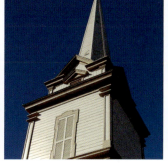

CHAPTER 1

The New Territory

The Territory of Nebraska was created with the passage of the Kansas-Nebraska Act of 1854, but by that time a few European-Americans were long settled into the Great Plains region. Fur traders were establishing trading posts along the Missouri River as early as 1812, and the federal government made a brief appearance with the establishment of Fort Atkinson on the river in 1820, but abandoned the post within seven years.

The Mormons began their migration to the Great Salt Lake in the 1840s and used the lands of Nebraska adjacent to the river as a starting point for their travel season. Enterprising people among the Mormons began a mill, and as others began to farm the "Great American Desert," as the plains were earlier termed, more mills were established to process the crops.

In a battle between those north of the Platte River and south of the river for dominance, Omaha successfully established itself as the territory's capital. Territorihood brought additional settlers, but not necessarily skilled builders and strong buildings—even the first territory capitol in Omaha had to be replaced after a few years. Among the first solid buildings was a church at the Indian mission in Bellevue and several bank buildings, primarily built to serve the speculators swarming into the territory. In the days of no federal regulation, many "wildcat" banks sprung up with only five in Bellevue, Brownville, Florence, Nebraska City, and Omaha having legislative support. A national panic in 1857 saw them close just as rapidly.

The Platte River was already seen as a transportation and communication channel to the west with the migrant trails. With the creation of the Pony Express more or less following the same route, several existing log structures along the way found additional life as stations for the riders.

The early settlements of Nebraska found varying degrees of success. Nebraska City became one of the most important towns in the territory as a shipping and transfer point between the Missouri and western trails. Its young and ambitious town leaders used Nebraska City's success to build a substantial edifice to their government.

This Bellevue log cabin likely started with the Presbyterian mission there.

Log Cabin • Bellevue

The first permanent European settlement in Nebraska began in 1823 with Peter Sarpy's American Fur Company trading post in what is now Bellevue. Local tradition has this log cabin being built around 1835, making it likely the oldest surviving building in Nebraska. By that time, Bellevue was an established Missouri River trading settlement of nearly twenty years, and this would have been one of its buildings. It was originally built on the river bottoms as a one-room, one-story structure, constructed of hand-hewn cottonwood logs with a central fireplace and an attic. Not long after its construction, a cholera outbreak caused its move from the river bottoms to an upper plateau, and in about 1850 it was moved to its present location at 1805 Hancock Street. Deed records show that the Presbyterian mission at Bellevue at that point was its owner, and Indians involved with the mission completed the move.

Serving as a private residence until 1854, a kitchen and pantry were added to the east side in 1906. The Sarpy County Historical Society, owner of the cabin, restored it to near-original appearance with a main floor restoration in 1972; a basement was added at that time, as well.

Weber Mill • Florence

The Weber Mill, in the northeast Omaha community of Florence, was built of timber in 1856 from a mill Mormons used during the 1840s Winter Quarters encampment. The mill's appearance evolved during its 150 years of flour production—interrupted for a short while in 1939, when periodic Missouri River flooding prompted the owner to move it to its current location. Now known as the Florence Mill, it is home to a museum of the history of the Mormons and the mill. Upstairs is an art gallery featuring the works of Nebraska artists, and in the summer months, a lively farmers market is held on the grounds.

The Weber Mill in Florence was built in 1856 with timber from an 1840s mill constructed by Mormons.

Bank of Florence • Florence

A few blocks away from the Florence Mill is the Bank of Florence, likely the oldest building in Omaha and one of two surviving "wildcat bank" buildings in the state (the Fontenelle Bank/County Courthouse building in Bellevue is the other). Founded in the speculative days of the Territory of Nebraska when it was allowed to print its own money, the redbrick building survived off and on as a bank through the 1930s, was once a telephone office, and hosted other businesses. The building bears some resemblance to Greek Revival commercial architecture, although it shows little ornamentation. Today, the building is home to the Florence Historical Foundation and its museum.

The Bank of Florence is one of two surviving "wildcat bank" buildings in the state.

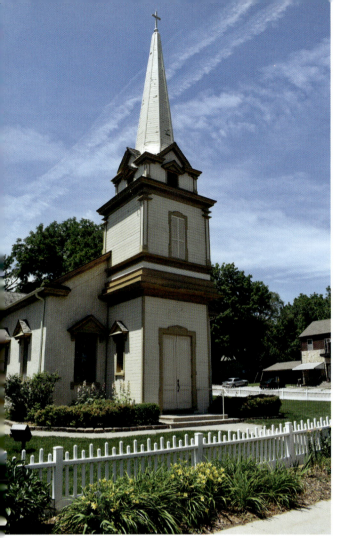

First Presbyterian Church • Bellevue

Constructed from 1856 to 1858, the First Presbyterian Church in Bellevue stands today as likely the oldest church building in Nebraska. Presbyterian missionaries first came to the area in the 1830s for the evangelization of Omaha and Otoe Indians, and a log building was originally built for services. The church was expanded in 1869 and doubled from its original size in 1904. Seating around five hundred, the church eventually proved too small for the congregation, which moved to a new building in 1959 after the centennial of its first home. Now owned by the Sarpy County Historical Society, it is one of the state's few buildings showing the Greek Revival style of architecture.

The First Presbyterian Church in Bellevue is probably Nebraska's oldest church building.

Once a fur trading post, the Midway Station had service as a Pony Express station.

Midway Station • Gothenburg

The Midway Station, located on the Lower 96 Ranch south of Gothenburg, has uncertain beginnings and perhaps an uncertain end. A plaque on the hand-hewn log structure gives the date of its construction as 1850 as a fur trading post on the Oregon Trail, although the National Register of Historic Places lists its construction at around 1859 and states that it later served as a Pony Express station in 1860–61, when two additions were made. One historical account states Indians destroyed the building by fire in 1866, yet the building stands today. A protective shed, not seen in the photo, was built over the building in recent years to protect it from the elements.

Nebraska's oldest public building, the Otoe County Courthouse in Nebraska City.

Otoe County Courthouse • Nebraska City

The Otoe County Courthouse in Nebraska City has the distinction of being the oldest public building in the state, and it has been in continuous use since its completion in 1864. The redbrick courthouse originally featured an Italianate style and consisted of just its center section, with an entrance tower facing the east and the downtown/Missouri River. A wing was added to the west around 1882 and an east wing in 1936. The result moved the entrance to the north, repositioned a new cupola to the building's center, and changed its character from Italianate to a classical Beaux-Arts design, although original elements—particularly its arched windows—were carried throughout the additions.

The US Post Office and Courthouse in Lincoln is one of the few buildings on the Great Plains with the High Victorian Gothic Revival style.

CHAPTER 2

The New State

1867 to 1879

Once Nebraska statehood was achieved in 1867, the more populous counties south of the Platte River immediately worked to remove the capital from Omaha. They exerted their political power and got the new state legislature to appoint a commission to site the new capital at a village called Lancaster, soon renamed Lincoln for the assassinated president. The legislature took the added step of centralizing the state university, state penitentiary, and other state institutions in the town, ensuring the growth and success of the new capital. Limestone from Gage County to the south was used to build the first state capitol, but shoddy design and construction meant its replacement would be soon.

By the time it lost the state capital, however, Omaha was already established as the economic capital of the state. It was a major shipping point on the Missouri River, had been named as the eastern terminus of the new transcontinental railroad, and would soon be the major conduit to the Platte as well. The Union Pacific and the Burlington railroads—developing as the state's two major rails—brought in hundreds of new residents. Its connection to eastern markets also made possible the establishment of the Sand Hills as a major cattle ranching area.

Homesteading continued at a rapid pace throughout the eastern part of the state as new settlers—often veterans of the Civil War—hoped to take advantage of the Homestead Act to build new lives as farmers. A farmer's success was determined by how close his horse and wagon were to the nearest town with a mill or elevator that would buy his crops, and the town's survival usually was set by its closeness to a railroad to ship them.

Towns of the frontier were quickly and cheaply built. In the early settlement of towns, commercial businesses usually ran parallel to the railroad tracks, with the rail depot as the center of activity. Each town of any size had the expected general store, blacksmith, hotel, livery stables, saloons, warehouse, bank, church, and school; county seats would have an attorney. Most of the businesses on the main streets were false-fronted wood-frame structures squeezed into a narrow lot, with little architectural statement to be made. Likewise, the homes in towns didn't reflect any adaptation to the prairie but were built to the standards of the eastern cities.

The Indian population was still significant in the new state, and for those who lived among the white settlers in the east, mission schools were built for their children's education. To the west, however, the War Department exerted its presence among the Indian tribes through the construction of military posts.

Nebraska faced several major crises during the 1870s—a national economic panic in 1873 hit the state hard, followed by a drought and a plague of grasshoppers that stripped the crops from 1874 through 1876. The threat of starvation very nearly took the state, but the return of rains in the late '70s brought a rebound of the economy and the promise of a new boom period.

The Palmer-Epard Cabin at Homestead National Monument was built in the first year of Nebraska statehood. The cabin was relocated on the monument's grounds from this site.

Palmer-Epard Cabin at Homestead National Monument • Beatrice

The Palmer-Epard Cabin, at Homestead National Monument near Beatrice, was built in 1867 from mixed hardwoods by George W. Palmer. The fourteen-by-sixteen-foot cabin was considered large and luxurious for its time, even with the Palmers having ten children. A ten-by-twelve-foot lean-to was added to the rear of the cabin sometime between 1875 and 1880, and the Palmers continued to live in it until 1895. They sold the cabin to nephew Eugene Mumford and William Foreman, who in turn sold it to other family members, Lawrence and Ida (Mumford) Epard, who lived in it for nearly forty years.

The cabin originally was about fourteen miles to the northeast of the national monument before it was moved here in 1950. National Park Service staff moved it in 1954 away from the highway and again in 1961 behind the Education Center (as pictured). During the fall of 2009, the cabin was moved to its present site behind the Heritage Center, surrounded by a restored tallgrass prairie.

Governor Robert W. Furnas House • Brownville

Robert W. Furnas was one of the early settlers to the Nebraska Territory, arriving in 1856 at the age of thirty-two and taking up residence in town of Brownville. Within two months, he began publication of the *Nebraska Advertiser* to advertise the territory's agricultural potential; in 1859, he founded the *Nebraska Farmer*, the state's first agriculture publication, which continues in print today.

Furnas was elected twice to the territory assembly, was a colonel in the territory militia during the Civil War, and was elected as the third governor of Nebraska, serving from 1873 to 1875. He was later the first president of the Nebraska State Historical Society, president of the State Horticultural Society and the State Board of Agriculture, and commissioner to expositions at Philadelphia, New Orleans, and Chicago.

Robert W. Furnas bought this 1868 Brownville home after his term as Nebraska's third governor.

Among the numerous Civil War–era buildings which survive in Brownville is the Governor Robert W. Furnas House, a two-and-a-half-story brick Gothic Revival/Italianate-style home originally built in 1868. Furnas bought and occupied it in 1878 after his term as governor. The house is now owned by the Nebraska State Historical Society Foundation and operated by the Brownville Fine Arts Association.

The 1869 Kennard House—the Nebraska Statehood Memorial—is Lincoln's oldest house.

Thomas P. Kennard House (Nebraska Statehood Memorial) • Lincoln

In 1867, the Nebraska state legislature appointed a commission to determine the site of the state capital. Its members—Governor David Butler, Auditor John Gillespie, and Secretary of State Thomas P. Kennard—named the village of Lancaster, soon renamed Lincoln, as the capital. The continuance of Lincoln as the capital was not assured, and there were efforts made to move the capital to another larger and established town, such as Kearney or Columbus.

To show their commitment to the site selected, the commissioners hired architect John K. Winchell of Chicago to design homes for each of them in Lincoln. Kennard's home was built in 1869, just a block away from the new capitol. Of the three houses, the Kennard House is the only to survive and is considered the oldest house in Lincoln.

In 1965, the Italianate house was named as the Nebraska Statehood Memorial under the direction of the Nebraska State Historical Society, which offers tours of the structure. As considerable modifications and style changes were made over its history, a restoration to its original appearance was made in 1968. Rather than recreate the home of Kennard, the restoration was to depict a Victorian family home of the 1870s.

The circa 1870 commanding officer's quarters at Fort Sidney include adobe walls covered in clapboard.

Fort Sidney • Sidney

As the transcontinental railroad rolled across the new state, military protection of the Union Pacific's work crews became a necessity. In 1867, a tent camp named Sidney Barracks was erected with a blockhouse as its one permanent building. Two years later, a permanent site for the post was located at the southeast corner of the town of Sidney and several wood-frame and adobe buildings were soon erected. The post was renamed Fort Sidney in 1874 to reflect its permanent status, and in years to come, a complex of forty buildings was developed.

The fort served the Nebraska frontier through the end of the Indian Wars and the Black Hills gold rush; its last major campaign was at Wounded Knee in 1890, where the fort's infantry troops participated. When the Army abandoned Fort Sidney in 1894, its buildings were auctioned off and became part of the Sidney town landscape.

Today, only three buildings survive. The commanding officer's quarters, built around 1870, represents one of the fort's first permanent structures and is the last building remaining from officers' row. The walls are of adobe construction covered by clapboard siding. The remaining two buildings are the octagonal 1872 powder magazine and the 1884 officers' quarters, now home of the Cheyenne County Museum.

Patterson Law Office • Central City

John Patterson, a native of Ireland, came to Nebraska after receiving his law degree from the University of Wisconsin in 1872. He immediately established a law practice in the town of Lone Pine (now Central City) and became a pioneer member of the bar in central Nebraska.

Patterson soon became a well-known trial lawyer and county attorney and also served as the superintendent of schools. He actively promoted the development of his town and county; two of his sons later joined him in his practice.

In the early days of Nebraska statehood, the one-story, false-front commercial building was common throughout town landscapes. Patterson was one of those constructing these buildings, and the 1872 Patterson Law Office building survives today as one of the oldest frame commercial buildings in Nebraska, predating most of the surviving nineteenth-century commercial buildings in the state by about twenty years. Located across from the Merrick County Courthouse in Central City, the building incorporates Greek Revival details in its design. Its simple detailing and street-scale proportions add to its example of this period.

Central City's Patterson Law Office is a false-front commercial building that was once common in Nebraska towns.

Freeman School at Homestead National Monument • Beatrice

The Freeman School at the Homestead National Monument is the best example of a one-room schoolhouse in Nebraska. Daniel Freeman and his neighbors built the school in 1872 using bricks made by a local landowner, Thomas Freeman (no relation). Succeeding farmers in the area kept their children in attendance and kept the doors open through the state's centennial in 1967, making it the longest-continually-operating school in Nebraska at one point. The redbrick school was also the focus of a successful lawsuit initiated by Freeman in the 1890s to stop religious instruction in the school.

Nebraska in 1918 had nearly seven thousand one-room schoolhouses. The vast majority were closed after the Great Depression by school consolidation; by 1986, only 385 were in operation. Still, that was the greatest number of any state in the country, with 45 percent of such schools. The last one-room schoolhouse in Nebraska was closed by 2012.

The Freeman School was restored by the National Park Service to its 1902 appearance in 1973–1975.

The 1872 Freeman School was one of thousands of one-room schoolhouses that dotted the rural landscape.

The Neligh Mill, today a state historic site, once produced flour for points as far as Europe.

Neligh Mill • Neligh

John D. Neligh was one of the first settlers of the town that bears his name, and in the same year of the town's founding—1873—he also started construction of the Neligh Mill on the Elkhorn River. Another settler bought the property and completed the construction in 1874. The new mill eventually grew to become the largest milling company in northeastern Nebraska, producing 140 barrels of flour daily. A government contract with the Indian Bureau and War Department led to Neligh flour being shipped to reservations and forts across the Plains. Orders went throughout the United States and as far as Europe, bringing twenty-four-hour production to the mill.

Flooding of the Elkhorn River eventually led to the abandonment of water power and the installation of diesel-powered electricity. World War II meant an increasing flour need, but it dropped off after the war, and the mill finally ended production in 1959. Ten years later, the Nebraska State Historical Society took over the Neligh Mill as a state historic site for the interpretation of the flour mill in the settlement and development of the state. The site includes the original 1873 redbrick mill, the 1886 warehouse, and the elevators built in 1886 and 1899. The Neligh Mill stands today as one of the best and largest examples of a water-powered mill in America.

Elijah Filley Stone Barn • Filley

Described as one of the most magnificent barns in Nebraska, the Elijah Filley Stone Barn—near the farmer's namesake town—is remarkable from a number of angles.

Elijah Filley's 1874 limestone barn displayed the farmer's confidence in Nebraska's future.

Elijah and Emily Filley first arrived at their Gage County farm in 1867 in Nebraska's statehood year and, after initially living in a tent, decided that they would stay. Using stone from a limestone outcrop on the property, Elijah's father Ammi quarried the stone, Emily hauled it to the site, and Elijah burned and laid the stone. The Filleys built their stone house on a hilltop, as earlier settlers had taken land close to wooded streams in valleys, but his hilltop farm ultimately proved to be more productive, and Filley soon became a prosperous farmer and stockman. The Panic of 1873 resulted in many area people out of work; as one of the few persons of means, Filley hired them to build his substantial limestone barn. Filley went on to become one of the most successful stockmen and community leaders of the area, and served in numerous public offices, including the Nebraska legislature.

As the surviving structure of Filley's Cottage Hill Farm, the barn is the largest limestone farm structure in the state, is an uncommon example of a barn built into an embankment, and is unusual in the use of arched openings and its overall aesthetically pleasing appearance. Filley's barn represented his confidence in the future of his farm and the state of Nebraska.

Fort Hartsuff, built in 1874, shows a then-rare use of grout, or concrete, as a construction medium.

Fort Hartsuff State Historical Park • Burwell

The US government built Fort Hartsuff in 1874 as a replacement for Fort Kearny and as a buffer between settlers of the North Loup Valley and the Sioux, who still occupied the Sand Hills. Like most forts on the frontier, it was constructed of materials locally available, and as the valley provided plenty of water, sand, gravel, and lime, Hartsuff was unique in its grout/concrete construction. Predicting the future more than he probably realized, the post commander said that concrete would become "the building material of the future."

As a result of its unique construction, Fort Hartsuff was considered one of the choice appointments within the Department of the Platte. The solid foot-thick walls blocked the winter winds and the summer heat of the plains better than most building material, and the uniform construction of the buildings made it one of the prettiest forts. The stability of the building material allowed the fort buildings to survive beyond its abandonment in 1884.

After years of neglect of the buildings—including some years as grain storage and animal shelter—the fort site was purchased, restored, and in 1961 incorporated into the state parks system. Little of the surrounding terrain has changed since its frontier days and Fort Hartsuff State Historical Park today represents among the best-preserved small prairie forts of the nineteenth-century Indian Wars.

Otoe-Missouria Mission School • Barneston

The Otoe Indians were formerly located on the Missouri River, but after a series of secessions to the US government were relocated onto 162,000 acres on the Big Blue River, south of Beatrice and on the Kansas border. The Otoe constructed about forty earth lodges, while a few agency buildings were constructed. Francis Barnes and his wife Mary Jane, who was half Otoe, settled on the new agency with the consent of the tribe; she ran a trader's store while he farmed. After continued white encroachment on the reservation, the Otoe relocated to Indian Territory (today's Oklahoma) in 1881. The post office name was changed from Otoe Agency to Barneston the previous year.

There's no question that the Otoe-Missouria Mission School building in Barneston was used for the education of Indian children on the tribe's Big Blue Reservation. The question is how it went from the three-story structure it was built as in 1874–75 to the two-story building it is today. There is a photo of the school building being dismantled, but it's not known if it was completely taken apart or whether a portion was actually converted into a farmhouse. Local residents saved it from total destruction and moved it in 1986 from its original site to its present location east of the Barneston town park. The nonprofit Otoe-Missouria Home Place at Barneston is now responsible for the building, presenting it as a link to the community's past.

Barneston's Otoe-Missouria Mission School is the sole surviving structure of the Otoe Agency in the state.

Dating to 1874, Fremont's Nye House owes most of its appearance to a post-1900 renovation.

Nye House • Fremont

Early Fremont settler and first mayor Theron Nye established himself in grain freighting, banking, lumber, and farming. He built for himself a two-story brick Italianate home in 1874 that he modified throughout the rest of his life. After his death in 1901, his son Ray employed the Milwaukee architectural firm of Ferry & Class (known for the Museum of Science and Industry Building at the 1893 Chicago World's Fair). They began a series of additions and alterations that turned the Nye House into a Georgian Revival mansion, a style popular throughout Nebraska at the turn of the century.

Ray Nye and his family occupied the home until 1921, when it was purchased by the Western Theological Seminary for a dormitory and classrooms. It was purchased by the Louis E. May Trust in 1968 for use as a county historical museum in Fremont, the present use of today's Nye House.

Columbus's 1876 Glur's Tavern is reportedly the oldest continually operating saloon west of the Mississippi.

Glur's Tavern • Columbus

Swiss immigrant brothers William and Joseph Bucher built their two-story saloon in 1876 for the refreshment of their fellow Columbus residents. William "Buffalo Bill" Cody was said to have been among those enjoying a drink or two at the tavern while in town in 1883 rehearsing for the world premiere of his Wild West Show in Omaha.

In 1925, William Bucher sold the saloon after nearly fifty years of ownership to longtime employee Louis Glur, who promptly renamed it Glur's Tavern. Glur maintained a European-like outdoor beer garden in addition to the tavern and hired traveling German bands to provide entertainment. When Prohibition forced the end of alcohol sales, he continued to run his saloon as a soft drink and ice cream parlor.

The tavern stands today as an active business and as the longest continually operating saloon west of the Mississippi. The simplified Italianate design has two additions to its rear but few alterations to the main structure, mostly around its L-shaped porch. Its original oak floors are still in place, as is its limestone foundation.

Fort Robinson Adobe Officers' Quarters • Crawford

Nearly seventy-five historic buildings line the grounds of Fort Robinson, an Indian Wars–era military post in the Pine Ridge which is today one of the prime attractions of the state park system. The oldest existing buildings at the fort are six identical adobe officers' quarters, one completed in 1874 as a prototype and the remainder in 1875. These buildings were in place for the greatest period of conflict between Indians and whites on the Northern Plains and witnessed some of its most exciting and tragic chapters on its own grounds, including the Cheyenne Outbreak and the death of Crazy Horse.

These buildings were erected on the original site of the fort, facing the old parade grounds. They were constructed of adobe bricks on sandstone foundations, using materials from the surrounding area. As adobe tends to "melt" in the northwest Nebraska climate, the bricks were protected with wood siding and porches. Intended for three officers each (with a company captain on one end and two lieutenants on the other), the quarters were cramped and provided virtually no space for dependents. Today, visitors to the state park may rent the quarters for truly historic lodging.

The 1874–75 adobe officers' quarters of Fort Robinson are the oldest buildings of the historic fort.

The 1879 Italianate General Crook House once hosted former President Ulysses S. Grant and President Rutherford B. Hayes as guests.

General Crook House • Omaha

In 1878, the Army shifted the headquarters of the Department of the Platte from offices in downtown Omaha to the ten-year-old Omaha Barracks (later Fort Omaha). The Army required department commander General George A. Crook and other officers to move to the post as well, leading to the construction of wood-frame officers' quarters and two-story redbrick quarters for Crook in 1879.

Italianate in style, the General Crook House (as it's known today) was the home for the general during two tours of duty in Omaha. Former President and Mrs. Ulysses S. Grant were guests in 1879 shortly after the house's opening, and President Rutherford B. Hayes reviewed troops from the porch the following year.

The house served as post quarters for various commanders over the years until Fort Omaha was deactivated as a military post and became a campus of Metropolitan Community College. Today, the General Crook House is the museum and offices of the Douglas County Historical Society.

The US Post Office and Courthouse in Lincoln is one of the few buildings on the Great Plains with the High Victorian Gothic Revival style.

US Post Office and Courthouse • Lincoln

The federal government built the US Post Office and Courthouse at 10th and O streets in downtown Lincoln between 1874 and 1879 from design completed by Alfred Mullet, the supervising architect of the US Treasury, and his successor William Appleton Potter. The project incorporated a High Victorian Gothic Revival/French Second Empire style, using brick faced with Nebraska limestone. The style used is considered very rare on the Great Plains, and it's not known if Potter carried out Mullet's plan or made substantial changes to the design. Potter only held the job for twelve months; today, he's better known for the churches he designed.

Architectural style aside, the building was important in the settlement of Nebraska as a US Land Office located here which processed the claims of five million acres of farmland in southern Nebraska from 1878 to 1906. After the completion of a new post office and courthouse in 1906, the federal government sold the building to the City of Lincoln. This became the city hall for Lincoln, used as such until 1969, when the new county/city building was complete. Because of the deed provisions, however, the City of Lincoln must continue to use the building for city-related activities or its ownership will revert to the federal government. The US Post Office and Courthouse/Old City Hall currently houses several Lincoln city offices.

Willa Cather House • Red Cloud

The Willa Cather House in Red Cloud is the childhood home of Pulitzer Prize–winning author Willa Cather. She lived in this house from 1884 to 1890, which she described as among the formative years in her writing career. Not unexpectedly, the home figures prominently in her books *The Song of the Lark*, *The Best Years*, and *Old Mrs. Harris*, and of the nearly two dozen buildings associated with Cather in Red Cloud, this one is seen as the most important to her literary life.

The house was built in 1878 with a simple, rectangular construction, but a later addition and covered porch gave it its L shape. Cather's parents lived in and rented the home through 1904, but even after they had moved and until they died, she visited them in Red Cloud every year and saw the home. The organization which became the Willa Cather Foundation purchased the home in 1960 from the descendants of its builder and restored and refurnished it to Cather's time, using personal items owned by her as well as her family's household items. The Childhood Home is managed by the Willa Cather Foundation and maintained by the Nebraska State Historical Society.

The childhood home of Willa Cather is prominently featured in three of the author's works.

Nebraska City's former US Post Office and Courthouse—now a bank—had a courtroom but probably never held any court proceedings.

CHAPTER 3

Building the West

The 1880s

The development of the ability to mass-produce steel directly led to the settlement of the Sand Hills country and its establishment as the state's most important cattle-grazing region. Wooden fences were impossible for the treeless plains, but the invention of steel barbed wire made the protection of gardens from cattle and the division of ranches possible. Steel production also led to the creation of windmills that could alter their facing with the wind, allowing ranches to tap into the abundant groundwater.

While technological advances meant agriculture and rural populations could advance, the populations of cities and towns also grew throughout the state. Nebraska was in a boom period in the 1880s; its population grew dramatically over a two-decade period, numbering 123,000 in 1870 and more than one million by 1890. Constant promotion by speculators and promoters for the settlement of the plains brought thousands to the communities via its railroads.

A wide variety of ethnic groups poured into the state's rural areas, mostly Germans, but also Czechs, Swedes, Danes, Poles, and Germans from Russia, forming small-town communities quite often centered around the church. Immigrants from the British Isles typically located in the larger cities.

The continuing rebound and prosperity of the economy meant Nebraskans could begin to reinvest in their communities. Some built larger and grander county courthouses, and others invested in higher education. Many of the private colleges and universities that exist in Nebraska today were founded in the 1870s and '80s, including Doane University (1872), Creighton University (1878), Hastings College (1882), Nebraska Wesleyan University (1887), Midland University (1883), and Clarkson College (1888). The private Omaha Medical College began in 1880 and is today's University of Nebraska Medical Center.

The University of Nebraska emerged in the 1880s as a true state university, with undergraduate and graduate programs, research and publication, recruitment and accreditation support for state high schools, and the establishment of colleges for agriculture, law, and teaching.

With its railroads, Omaha expanded as the center of commerce in taking, processing, and shipping the state's agricultural products. Beef, grain, dairy products, beer, and whiskey translated to stockyards, meatpacking plants, creameries, grain elevators, flour mills, breweries, and distilleries for the city. National companies like Anheuser-Busch and New York Life Insurance chose the city for regional operations.

In the boom of the 1880s, the rich of the state became richer and many built mansions, some of which survive today. This was also the decade in which a celebrity Army scout from North Platte built a new type of entertainment—a Wild West show—which put him on the path to becoming the world's first superstar.

The 1884 McCormick Building has always played an active role on the Hastings College campus.

McCormick Hall • Hastings College

Since the early 1870s, the citizens of Hastings had planned for a college in their town, but drought, grasshoppers, and economic downturns delayed its organization. Finally, in 1882, a site was purchased east of town for the new college, to be affiliated with the Presbyterian church, and construction began on its first building in 1883.

McCormick Hall was dedicated in the fall of 1884, named for American inventor Cyrus H. McCormick, who contributed the first $5,000 for the two-story Italianate brick building with a three-story entrance. From its opening through the 1950s, the building was the main classroom building and home of the departments of English, mathematics, speech, drama, and chemistry. The building still rests on its original limestone foundation and continues to host classroom space today, with virtually every Hastings College student having had at least one course in the building. McCormick Hall is an outstanding example of an educational architecture-type building of the late nineteenth century that was once common but is rare today.

Trinity Episcopal Cathedral • Omaha

Episcopalians organized Trinity Parish in 1856, just two years after the founding of Omaha. Twelve years later, it was named as the bishop's church, earning the designation of a cathedral.

The present cathedral was completed in 1883 after a three-year building process. It was designed by Henry G. Harrison, an English architect who planned it in the Late Gothic Revival architecture emphasizing the English Perpendicular style, all of which is seen in the masonry walls, stone bar tracery, monochrome coloring, and its uncomplicated plan. An Omaha architect, Alfred Dufrene, supervised the construction, as Harrison never came to Omaha.

The cathedral follows a cruciform plan with the addition of a single tower, which also serves as the main entrance and as an easily visible identifier to traffic on its intersecting street corner. The interior of the church is also Gothic in appearance, although its wooden beams vault straight across the ceiling and not in the traditional vault form.

Trinity was the home church for many of the pioneer families of Omaha, and their contributions are seen in many of its spectacular stained-glass windows. One of its more unusual windows is a dedication to Major Thomas T. Thornburgh, killed in an Indian Wars battle in Colorado and whose wife's family lived in Omaha; part of the memorial is a crossed-cannons-with-flags panel, reflecting his artillery service in the Civil War.

Trinity Episcopal Cathedral was the home church for many of the pioneer families of Omaha.

The 1885 Phelps Hotel in Big Springs continues to provide lodging for travelers.

Phelps Hotel • Big Springs

To provide lodging for railroad workers of the nearby Union Pacific, the Phelps Hotel was built in Big Springs in 1885 by the Edwin A. Phelps family, one of the earliest settlers in the vicinity. The hotel was built as a large, unpretentious, two-story frame structure with a full basement and a hipped roof. The lower story included an office, parlor, dining room, kitchen, and bedroom, while the upper story was divided into ten bedrooms.

Often called "The House of Three Chimneys" in its early days, it is the oldest hotel in Deuel County and is typical of many hotels built in western Nebraska during the late nineteenth century. It catered to the many homesteaders, travelers, and pioneers entering the area, and also served as a house of worship when church services were held there. Phelps's wife Sarah operated the hotel after her husband's death, and then Edwin Phelps Jr. and his wife ran it until 1965. The building was vacant for many years, but today is operated as a bed and breakfast.

Buffalo Bill's house at his Scout's Rest Ranch duplicated another house which once stood in North Platte.

Cody House at Scout's Rest Ranch • North Platte

The home of William F. "Buffalo Bill" Cody at his Scout's Rest Ranch was built in 1886 under the direction of his sister, Julia (Cody) Goodman. She was not the architect—she simply chose to pattern it exactly after the home of a judge in nearby North Platte. The same carpenter-contractor for that house was hired for the work in building this duplicate, a two-story frame house derived of the French Second Empire style with Italianate and Eastlake features. The only alteration asked by Cody was for a ten-foot-wide porch instead of the traditional six feet.

The Second Empire features are seen in the mansard roof, dormer windows, and three-story tower. The irregular massing of the features is typical of the Second Empire style. The two-story bay window and brackets of the cornice are suggestive of the Italianate influence, and the large front porch draws from the Eastlake influence.

The Cody family last lived in the house in 1913. After various owners, the house had fallen into significant disrepair by the time the State of Nebraska took ownership in 1960. The Nebraska Game and Parks Commission established the home and grounds as a state historical park and began a major structural and interior renovation of the house from 1962 to 1964, with new steel I beams and poured concrete footings and the removal, cleaning, and reuse, where possible, of the original shingle siding, railings, and details.

Anheuser-Busch Office Building • Omaha

The Anheuser-Busch Office Building in downtown Omaha was built in 1887 as part of a complex of buildings for the beer brewing company and distributor. Henry Voss, an Omaha architect and German immigrant, designed the site for the St. Louis brewer as a complex that included a stable, beer vault/ice house, and bottling facility, all of which are gone today.

The surviving office building, however, was the gem of the redbrick complex and is considered one of the

The 1887 Anheuser-Busch Office Building is considered an elaborate example of the Romanesque Revival style.

most elaborate examples of the Romanesque Revival style in the city. Its high ceilings and raised basement gave it a slight height advantage over the cross-alley stable, but also featured much more ornamentation than the other buildings, with its cut stone trim and copper coping, finials, and wall cornice. After the distributorship closed in 1916, a number of other concerns occupied the building, including an industrial chemical company, a furniture-stripping business, and individuals who used it as a private residence. In 1988, the Alley Poyner architecture firm renovated the interior space and used the building as its offices.

Brandhoefer Mansion • Ogallala

Known and promoted as "The Mansion on the Hill," the Brandhoefer Mansion is a prominent Ogallala landmark. Leonidas A. Brandhoefer, originally from Pennsylvania, came to Nebraska in the early 1870s and started a lumber business in York. He sold the company and moved to Ogallala in 1885, hiring on as cashier at the local Bank of Ogallala. He began construction on the Italian Renaissance mansion at a site overlooking the town a year after his arrival, becoming one of the first to bring a popular Eastern residential style to the Western settlements. Brandhoefer used a locally fired brick, the same used in the original Keith County Courthouse.

The banker never had the chance to occupy his new home. Shortly before its completion in 1887, Brandhoefer was struck by a paralytic infliction which forced his return to York to convalesce. He later resigned from the bank, and the resulting financial struggles forced the sale of his home in 1888. The mansion passed through several owners before the Keith County Historical Society's purchase and restoration in 1966, when it was rededicated as the county's historical museum in Nebraska's centennial year.

The Brandhoefer Mansion has nine rooms, with ten-foot ceilings on the first-floor rooms and exterior walls of sixteen-inch thickness. It has two bathrooms, which was highly unusual for the time period and region of Nebraska. The exterior Queen Anne wood cornice details and cast-iron ornamentation complete its Victorian character.

The Brandhoefer Mansion was one of the first homes in western Nebraska with the popular Italian Renaissance style.

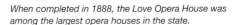
When completed in 1888, the Love Opera House was among the largest opera houses in the state.

Love-Larson Opera House • Fremont

James Wheeler Love commissioned Omaha architect Francis M. Ellis to design his downtown Fremont opera house in 1888. It was immediately considered one of the finest buildings in Nebraska with its unique three-part vertical block architectural design and trims of stone and pressed metal cornices and ornaments. It was also among the largest opera houses in the state, with a capacity of 1,100 within five stories (basement included).

Love's daughter sold it in 1903 to L. P. Larson, who renamed it for himself and continued to offer live entertainment such as minstrel shows, musical concerts, and stage plays for Fremont. Larson made several large, cosmetic changes to the interior, which increased the performing space but reduced its seating. The opera house era ended for Fremont (as well as most of Nebraska) by the 1920s as movie theaters and a new auditorium provided entertainment and large venue space. The Larson Opera House held events only occasionally and eventually was closed.

In 1975, the opera house became the first Fremont property to join the National Register of Historic Places in recognition of its architecture, its size, and its historic past. A local nonprofit corporation, Friends of the Fremont Opera House, was organized to preserve the historic building as a performing arts and community center and continues to host events there while also continuing the building's redevelopment.

Omaha Building • Omaha

Nebraska's first "skyscraper" was a ten-story building constructed in downtown Omaha for the New York Life Insurance Company to house its local office. Construction started in 1887 (about the same time as an identical building for the firm in Kansas City, which still stands today) and was completed in 1889, instantly becoming one of the most prominent landmarks of the frontier city.

Designed by Stanford White of the New York architectural firm of McKim, Mead and White, the imposing yet elaborate building is detailed with elements of Classical architecture. It was derived from the Florentine palazzo, with rusticated granite below and brick and terra-cotta above. A large bronze eagle designed by the Beaux-Arts sculptor Louis Saint-Gaudens is positioned above the high arched main entrance. This is among the last buildings to make use of the massive masonry bearing walls for tall buildings, as the iron skeleton frame became the norm in 1890, followed by the high-strength steel of today.

The Omaha National Bank purchased the building in 1909 as its main branch and added an additional floor in 1920. The law firm of Kutak Rock—once a tenant of the Omaha Building in the 1960s—purchased the now-abandoned structure in 1976 as its new home. The firm has twice renovated the building's interior in its more than forty years of ownership—in 1977 and in 2006–07—maintaining its grandeur through the years.

Originally built as a regional office of the New York Life Insurance Company, the Omaha Building survives today as the city's oldest skyscraper.

The Johnson County Courthouse is a prime example of the Property-type "County Capitol" in Nebraska.

Johnson County Courthouse •
Tecumseh

Johnson County in 1857 was one of the first counties established in the Territory of Nebraska. Its county seat of Tecumseh was platted in 1856, built its first courthouse in 1857, and replaced it in 1868. The county enjoyed a period of prosperity in the 1880s and its voters in 1888 passed a bond issue to build a courthouse that made a statement. Construction began the same year and the Romanesque Revival-style building was completed in 1889.

The courthouse is a prime example of the Property-type "County Capitol," the oldest among eighteen existing examples in Nebraska. It's noted for its corner towers and central dome, permanent and costly materials, elaborate ornamentation, four entrances, and an impression of a government building of permanence and strength. It was designed by noted Lincoln-based architect William Gray, who is known to have submitted plans for nine other Nebraska courthouses and was selected for five (Johnson, Cass, Hamilton, Butler, and York). It was intended to duplicate the since-demolished York courthouse. Gray used cherry-red St. Joseph brick to contrast against the Nemaha County limestone, which was variously rough-cut, smoothed, and carved.

The Johnson County Courthouse had a bit role in Hollywood, as a site location in the made-for-TV miniseries *Amerika*.

US Post Office and Courthouse • Nebraska City

W. E. Bell, the supervising architect for the US Treasury, directed the design of the Nebraska City US Post Office and Courthouse in 1886, creating an outstanding example of late-nineteenth-century governmental architecture. The two-story structure is built of locally fired brick and combines elements of the Chateauesque and Romanesque Revival styles. Congress appropriated additional funds during construction to nearly double the size of the building. Immediately noticed are the story-high turrets at each corner of the building and elaborate half-round arches at the building entrances.

The building was used as a post office from its beginning, and was the longest continually operated federal building and post office in Nebraska until the construction of a new facility in the 1980s. There's no evidence that the building was ever used for court proceedings, in spite of the available courtroom space.

Nebraska City's former US Post Office and Courthouse—now a bank—had a courtroom but probably never held any court proceedings.

In 1988, the Nebraska City–based Farmers Bank did a restoration and renovation of the building as its new home. The building was virtually unchanged for the entirety of its existence, and holds a greater architectural significance as a result. In Nebraska history, it holds the distinction of being the first post office in the state to offer free mail delivery in 1887–1889 and the first rural free delivery in 1901.

The Frank House was one of the first west of the Missouri River to be wired for electricity.

Frank House • Kearney

George W. Frank established the first canal/water supply to Kearney, envisioning it as the first necessary step in turning the town into an industrial center. A building boom did take place and Frank acted on this success by taking space for an estate in an exclusive west Kearney suburb.

The 1889 home was designed by his son, George William Frank Jr., an architect with the Kearney firm of Frank, Bailey & Farmer. It was built in the Richardsonian Romanesque/Shingle style with Colorado red sandstone, one of the earliest examples of the styles in Nebraska. The roof, typical of the Shingle style, forms a veranda along the entire length of the main façade. The massive dormer projections are also typical, but the use of imported tile was an effective departure from the usual wood shingles. This was a spectacular home for Kearney; it was one of the first west of the Missouri River to be wired for electricity.

Frank's canal failed to keep up with Kearney's boom, and unpowered factories were forced to close. That, along with a national economic downturn and a drought in Nebraska, ultimately forced the Franks to sell their home in 1900. A series of other owners occupied the home until it was sold to the State of Nebraska for use as the staff home of the Nebraska State Tuberculosis Hospital. Kearney State College (now the University of Nebraska at Kearney) acquired the house in 1971; it is now a museum for the university.

The Rock Island Depot in Lincoln is Nebraska's only rail station of the Chateauesque/Francois I architectural style.

Wealth to Build

The 1890s

Although a drought and recession dominated much of the 1890s and stopped much construction, the boom of the 1880s carried over into the early years as many Nebraska counties continued to express their success through their courthouses. Nearly a tenth of the state's "County Capitols" that stand and serve today were built in this time period, including those in Gage, Nuckolls, Jefferson, Cherry, Cass, Fillmore, Antelope, and Hamilton counties.

Prominent architects were hired to design solid, massive, richly detailed edifices to government, using new popular styles from the East and from Europe. These were built at considerable expense—not only to show off, but sometimes to head off any voter action to move the county seat from one town to another.

Nebraska was passing from the frontier. Its sophistication in building was shown beyond the government buildings to other public-use spaces. The Rock Island Line built a beautiful new depot in the capital city of Lincoln in the 1890s, and the City of Omaha hired a promising young architect named Thomas Rogers Kimball to design a stunning new city library that evoked the great libraries of the East. The University of Nebraska at Lincoln continued its growth and influence with the construction of a new library of its own. The town hotels also became town centers for meeting and dining in addition to lodging; the Hotel Wilber was one reflecting the "restrained elegance" of these buildings.

Fraternal groups continued to form and exert their influence in the state, but perhaps none were stronger at this time than the Grand Army of the Republic. These veterans of the Civil War initially joined for camaraderie but soon became a voting arm of the Republican Party and ensured its success in elections for generations.

Of course, homes continued to be built throughout the towns of Nebraska, some of which would become homes of great names in the state's future.

The return of rains and a rebound in the economy did allow for one more architectural statement before the end of the century—the buildings of the Trans-Mississippi and International Exposition in Omaha. Although the buildings were constructed of plaster and lathe and intended to be temporary, the designs created by Thomas Kimball gave him national prominence.

One of the state's finest courthouses, the 1891 Jefferson County Courthouse, incorporates a variety of styles, textures, materials, and forms.

Jefferson County Courthouse • Fairbury

One of the state's finest, the 1891 Jefferson County Courthouse in Fairbury incorporates the popular Richardsonian Romanesque style of the latter nineteenth century. The times were prosperous for the counties such as Jefferson, and quite often their leaders expressed their county pride through their new courthouse construction.

The design was submitted by Topeka, Kansas, architect J. C. Holland and was built at a time when the profession showed more eclecticism in its work. He took advantage of the times and the generous budget ($60,000) to create a courthouse with a variety of styles, textures, materials, and forms. The building is constructed of rusticated limestone (hand-cut by brothers Arthur and Ferdinand Bower, who had immigrated to Fairbury from England) with cornice and window detailing on smooth-faced stone. Ornate roof structures with false dormers cap the corners, giving a Victorian feel to what is an otherwise classic Romanesque feature. In 1910, the county added a clock to all four faces of the coppered capitol tower-cupola.

Cass County Courthouse • Plattsmouth

Like the courthouse of Johnson County, the Cass County Courthouse was built in 1891–92 by Nebraska architect William Gray in the County Capitol style with Romanesque Revival detailing. Unlike that courthouse, however, the expensive Plattsmouth structure was built to help ensure the Missouri River town wasn't lost as county seat to a more centrally located community as the county's population spread west.

The Cass County Courthouse's County Capitol style as usual incorporates the massing of a central tower and corner towers, fine materials, and detailed decorating. In fact, it's difficult to find a surface of the courthouse that isn't

The Cass County Courthouse was built in 1891–92 to spend a high budget in large part to undercut efforts to move the seat to a more central spot in the county.

trimmed. Terra-cotta is used at the apex of each tower's gable, which is above smooth stone, then above brick, and then above an arched window or clock face. There are checkerboards of smooth and rough-cut stone, buttresses of terra-cotta with foliated tops, and quilted shafts and wall surfaces.

Unusual for the County Capitol style, however, is that the courthouse is not constructed in a central square but on half of a city block with only two entrances—on the west and south sides—leading to an L-shaped office configuration. Further complicating the traditional design is that the courthouse is built on a hillside, with the main entrance spilling down a concrete walk to Plattsmouth's Main Street.

Champion Mill • Champion

With the conversion of the Chase County economy from ranching to farming, construction began on Frenchman River for a new flour mill in 1886 that was in full production by 1888. That mill, located in the southwest Nebraska town of Champion, was destroyed by a fire in the early 1890s but rebuilt in 1892. Besides milling flour and feed, its mill pond became a community recreational destination for fishing, boating, swimming, skating, and picnicking. The mill closed in 1968 and was sold to the Nebraska Game and Parks Commission; it had been the longest operating functional water powered mill in the state.

The NGPC operated the property as a state historical park from 1969 to 2013, when it then transferred ownership to Chase County for public use. Very little of the original appearance and setting of the mill has changed. Champion Mill consists of three buildings, incorporated under one roof. The original 1892 mill is a three-story wood-frame structure which makes up its middle portion; a two-story storeroom was added in 1918, and in 1929, a third-floor addition was made to the mill. A one-and-three-quarter-story office with a shop was added to the mill in 1915, a one-story turbine house in 1929, and a boiler room in 1945. The entire structure was re-shingled and re-sided due to deterioration, using cedar shingles and cedar horizontal bevel siding, using like materials as were originally used.

Champion Mill was once the longest operating functional water-powered mill in Nebraska.

The Rock Island Depot in Lincoln is Nebraska's only rail station of the Chateauesque/Francois I architectural style.

Rock Island Depot • Lincoln

When the Chicago, Rock Island and Pacific Railroad completed its line through Nebraska's capital city in 1893, it also constructed a showpiece passenger station.

Lincoln's Rock Island Depot is probably the best of the state's rail stations still in existence from the nineteenth century and the only of the Chateauesque/Francois I architectural style, introduced from France in the late 1800s. Constructed of Colorado red sandstone and pressed brick, the building stands out sharply with its steeply pitched slate roofs. The station isn't particularly large, but does have prominence with its O Street location, Lincoln's main street. The identity of the structure's architect isn't clearly known, although plans for the building were completed under Rock Island's chief engineer, R. W. Day, with Eugene Woerner of Lincoln as the contractor.

The Rock Island ended passenger service in 1966 and the station was closed. In 1968, Clark Enerson Partners architects restored and adapted the station as the branch of a bank, supposedly the first such conversion in America and one of Nebraska's most successful examples of a "living" restoration. The structure continues as a bank today and is virtually unchanged in appearance, as few alterations were made over the years.

Wright Morris Boyhood Home • Central City

"The house in which I spent my childhood, and remains the center of all my boyhood impressions, is on the southwest corner of B and D, across from the Baptist Church," wrote Wright Morris. "I confess I feel a great attachment for it."

Morris, who went on to become one of the state's and the nation's most gifted writers as winner of both the National Book Award and American Book Award, frequently drew upon his Nebraska childhood in his works. He was born in 1910 at Central City, where his father worked for the Union Pacific Railroad, the tracks of which are but one block from the home. Morris's mother died six days after he was born and he was raised by a nanny. His father remarried and the family moved to Omaha in 1919.

Morris lived in several different houses in Central City while growing up. He requested in 1979 that one of them be preserved as his boyhood home, and chose the house where he had his best memories. It has been furnished to the time of his youth and is maintained by the Lone Tree Literary Society.

The one-story wood-frame home was built in 1893 by W. C. Kerr, owner of a real estate, loan, and insurance company. It is a T-shaped structure featuring gabled wall dormers and two enclosed rear porches, with the gablets repeated in the window and door trims.

This Central City home was selected by Wright Morris for preservation as his boyhood home.

Omaha Public Library • Omaha

The former Omaha Public Library is considered to be one of the city's most impressive architectural landmarks, designed by probably the most prolific and noted architect in Nebraska history. Thomas Rogers Kimball designed the Second Renaissance Revival structure in 1891 for completion in 1893. This was the young architect's first major commission and came when he was partner with the Boston firm of Walker & Kimball, with Kimball running its Omaha office. The most prominent example of the Second Renaissance Revival style is McKim, Mead and White's Boston Public Library, elements of which are recognizable in the Omaha building. Kimball was living in Boston during the design and construction of that library and obviously was impressed.

The Omaha architect was working at a much smaller scale than the Boston library, however. He thus put more emphasis on the entrance and used tall, rectangular windows on the first floor to give the impression of height in what is otherwise a horizontal building. The windows draw the eye upward to a second floor of arched windows, which in turn draws attention to the third floor and its corniced roofline. Here Kimball installed a series of high-relief medallions featuring important ancient figures such as Caesar, Sophocles, Homer, Aristotle, and Plato. The study of the medallions then draws the attention back to the arched windows, each of which has the name of a prominent author—Dante, Shakespeare, Longfellow, and ten others. The detailing gave the impression of an Italian Renaissance palazzo and fell in with the City Beautiful movement taking place across the Midwest.

After the construction of a new downtown library in 1977, the old public library was converted to office space in 1982, with the exterior walls, roundels, copper roof, and interior iron staircase among the major features restored to original condition.

The former Omaha Public Library was the first major commission of architect Thomas R. Kimball.

Nebraska City's GAR Hall is a remnant of a once influential fraternal group. It is now a Civil War museum.

GAR Memorial Hall •
Nebraska City

Lured by the promise of land through the Homestead Act of 1862, hundreds of Union veterans streamed into Nebraska in the 1860s and 1870s. Most of those men joined the Grand Army of the Republic (GAR), a fraternal organization which became a political advocacy group for veterans' pensions and promoting patriotism education. Its peak membership came in 1890, when there were more than 490,000 in the United States, wielding considerable influence both locally and nationally. Many Nebraska towns were founded by veterans.

More than 370 posts were formed by local veterans in Nebraska, around one hundred of which had meeting halls. Three of these halls were built as freestanding structures, the most prominent of which is the GAR Memorial Hall in Nebraska City in which a high degree of its external and interior integrity remain. Built in 1894 and designed by the Omaha firm of Fisher & Lawrie, the building is in the Richardsonian Romanesque style. The Col. William Baumer Post No. 24 and other community organizations met here through 1932, when a new memorial building was constructed; the post itself disbanded in 1934, but other groups continued to use the hall.

A nonprofit organization was formed in 1991 to restore and preserve the GAR Memorial Hall. Today, the building is home to the Civil War Veterans Museum, containing artifacts relating to the GAR and the Civil War.

Hotel Wilber • Wilber

Most small towns in Nebraska by the end of the nineteenth century had a hotel, not only for travelers but also as a social center for local citizens. As the county seat of Saline County, the town of Wilber built a substantial two-story brick hotel for that purpose.

The Hotel Wilber was constructed as a first-class property with a large office and lobby, along with a front and back parlor with family rooms. A small lobby was set on the second floor, central to east-west and north-south hallways leading to twenty rooms. A large dining room had seating for fifty.

The architect of the building isn't known today, but his work demonstrates the restrained elegance sought for these lodges. Most of the building features the stilted, segmented arch typically seen on structures of this era, but the street-side windows and doors feature rough-cut stone lintels and sills.

The two-story columned porches and pressed-metal gable contribute to the impression of luxury.

The hotel closed in the 1960s, but a nonprofit organization, Nebraska Czechs of Wilber, has since taken over the building and restored it as a bed and breakfast. The Hotel Wilber stands today as an example of the once-common-but-swiftly-fading small-town hotel.

The Hotel Wilber demonstrates the restrained elegance sought for these well-used town structures.

This small, one-room house provided basic shelter for a few families but is better remembered as the study of poet laureate John G. Neihardt.

John G. Neihardt Study • Bancroft

"This is where I had the big dreams and where they began to come true," is how Nebraska poet laureate John G. Neihardt remembered the little house he rented as a study, across the alley from his residence in Bancroft. From the years of 1911 to 1921, Neihardt used the small dwelling to begin his most well-known, ambitious, and important work, *A Cycle of the West*. This collection of epic poems telling the story of the exploration and settlement of the Trans-Missouri West established Neihardt as one of the foremost American poets of the twentieth century.

Neihardt's study was probably erected in the early 1890s by August Hartman as a home for his daughter and her husband. The house provided basic shelter—it was a one-story wood-frame structure with one room and a veranda porch. The Canarsky family of Bancroft bought it around 1900; they owned and occasionally occupied it until 1964. The Bancroft Commercial Club then bought the property, reselling it to the John G. Neihardt Foundation in 1968. The study is now part of the Nebraska State Historical Society's John G. Neihardt State Historic Site, which includes a museum/visitor center in addition to the study. The Society has furnished the small house as Neihardt may have during his occupancy.

Senator George W. Norris House • McCook

The Senator George W. Norris House in McCook commemorates the Nebraskan who became one of America's most noted statesmen. Over the course of forty years in the US House and Senate, Norris sponsored passage of the Twentieth Amendment, was the force behind the passage of the Rural Electrification Act and the Tennessee Valley Authority, and in Nebraska, led the establishment of Nebraska's unicameral legislature, the only such representative body in the United States. A panel of 160 scholars in 1957 named him as the top choice for the five best senators in US history.

Norris and his wife bought the home in 1899, when they moved to McCook from Beaver City, Nebraska. The two-story, eight-room house was built sometime in the 1890s by a Mr. Harris, a division superintendent with Burlington Railroad. Norris's wife died in 1901; he remarried in 1903. They remodeled the home in 1930–31 and stuccoed it a dark gray color (it has been repainted several times and is currently a light gray). Norris lived in the home until his death in 1944, and his widow continued to make it her home. In 1968, the Norris family donated the property to the State of Nebraska. It is operated today as a branch museum of the Nebraska State Historical Society.

George Norris bought this house in 1899. His family donated it to the state nearly seventy years later.

Originally constructed as the University of Nebraska library, Architecture Hall has been home to the architecture department since 1947.

Architecture Hall • Lincoln

The oldest building on the University of Nebraska–Lincoln campus is its former library, the present Architecture Hall. Built in 1895, it is the only nineteenth-century building on the campus and the only one that evokes the university's beginnings in the Victorian era.

Designed by Mendelssohn, Fisher & Lawrie from Omaha, the Richardsonian Romanesque building is constructed of Colorado sandstone on concrete footings. The upper floors were specified for "selected, hard burned, cherry red brick laid wet." The first floor was once the home of the Nebraska State Historical Society and its ten-thousand-volume library, while the second floor served as the university library (the Society moved out in 1912). The third floor contained an art gallery and classrooms for mechanical and freehand drawing.

Continued growth of the library collection led to the construction of the new Love Library on the university campus and the transfer of the collection to it in 1941. The former library was Navy Hall for a short while in the late 1940s, but in 1947 the structure became Architecture Hall as the new home of the architecture department.

A major renovation took place in 1985–1987 to link Architecture Hall and the old Law College through the creation of a glass connector. The exterior of the renovated building is basically unchanged from its original form, with the exception being the loss of a chimney on the northeast corner of the north wing.

Thomas Rogers Kimball's St. Cecilia Cathedral took more than fifty years to complete and was one of the nation's ten largest cathedrals.

CHAPTER 5

The New Century

The 1900s

With the new century, Nebraska was transitioning from the frontier and adapting to the cultural shifts taking place in the rest of America, and this was reflected in its architecture.

The Indian Wars ended in the 1890s and the US policy of forced assimilation continued for Native Americans. Many of the tribal youth were sent to non-reservation boarding schools—including one in Nebraska—for instruction in European-American culture and vocational skills.

The Union Pacific and Burlington railroads expanded their networks across the state, adding more than two thousand miles to their reach in the first decade of the new century. In providing service to hundreds of passengers, the railroads built impressive new depots. For the design of its new depot in Hastings, the Burlington hired Thomas Rogers Kimball, who had already impressed the world for three years as lead architect of the Trans-Mississippi and International Exposition.

This new century heralded the "decade of Kimball." The Omaha architect was already established as a great Nebraska architect, but these ten years would place him among the nation's preeminent designers. Throughout the state, Kimball displayed an incredible range and productivity in buildings for education, government, commerce, transportation, and communications, in addition to many residences. Kimball was about to impress even more as the architect of the new St. Cecilia Cathedral in Omaha. Started in 1905 and completed more than fifty years later, his dramatic departure from traditional cathedrals further established him as one of the country's most relevant architects.

Nebraskans began to settle western Nebraska and the Sand Hills with passage of the Kinkaid Act, authored by Nebraska Congressman Moses P. Kinkaid of O'Neill, which gave 640 acres of land to settlers who improved upon the property. Many continued the folk-architecture practice of building their home of sod.

The hard life of farming and relative prosperity of the decade brought a desire for more entertainment, and for many communities it was the Chautauqua. Bringing musicians, lecturers, politicians, and sermons to the masses, some communities like Beatrice and Hastings built large pavilions to house the events. By far the most popular (and best paid) was William Jennings Bryan of Lincoln, who built himself a stunning new home with the returns of his success.

Nebraskans found success in a number of fields and shared it through their mansion homes. The wealthy son of J. Sterling Morton turned his family home into a shrine, George Joslyn's fortune from newspapers built a castle, and a couple from McCook took a chance on an innovative young architect named Frank Lloyd Wright.

The unique construction of the sod Dowse House near Comstock has kept it standing for well over a century.

Dowse House • Comstock

Settlers typically build homes from the natural materials on hand, but on the treeless plains of Nebraska—which were also devoid of natural stone—the preferred medium was the ground under their feet. Hundreds of Nebraskans built their first homes of sod bricks when they moved to the area, and "soddies" (as they came to be nicknamed) were everywhere. They were swiftly built (typically within a week) and cost less than five dollars for materials. They provided coolness in the summer and warmth in the winter, and even withstood winds better than frame houses. Ethnic groups from the Irish to Czechs to German-Russians all adapted the use of sod for shelter.

The William R. Dowse House southwest of Comstock was one of these homes. Built in 1900 and occupied until 1959, it is a true survivor. Most sod houses crumbled over time and in the often severe Nebraska climate. This is one of the few standing "soddies" in the state, in large part because of its unique construction. Dowse, a farmer, built his home in an L shape with three rooms divided by partitions, leading to greater stability; a hipped roof also contributed to its stability. The Dowses continued to make improvements to the house to extend its life beyond the norm, such as plastering the exterior walls with a clay/straw/hog hair mixture and later with concrete. The house sat abandoned for more than two decades until descendants of William Dowse and the Comstock community restored the house in the 1980s. It is presented today as an excellent example of the sod house phenomenon.

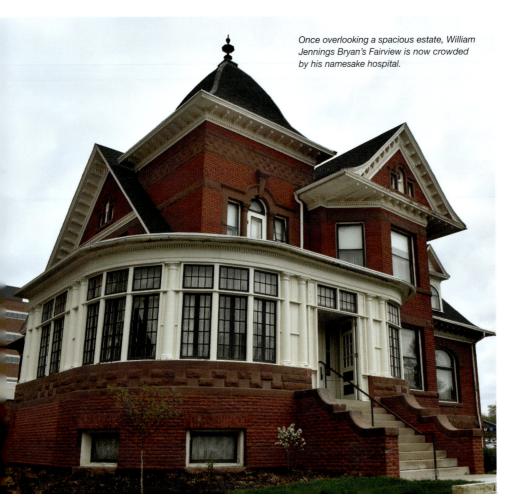

Once overlooking a spacious estate, William Jennings Bryan's Fairview is now crowded by his namesake hospital.

Fairview (William Jennings Bryan Home) • Lincoln

Orator and national political figure William Jennings Bryan hired Lincoln architect Artemis A. Roberts to build his new Lincoln home in 1902. "The Great Commoner"—as he was called by the national press—had lost his second run for the presidency two years earlier was perhaps looking for a place to reflect on his career and consider options for his future at his east-of-Lincoln farm. With its commanding western view of Antelope Creek and the growing city of Lincoln, the farm and home were named "Fairview."

Roberts designed the one-and-a-half-story redbrick home with a combination of the popular Queen Anne and Classic Revival styles. The structure features a slate roof with numerous gables and dormers, a tower with a bell-cast pyramid roof, cornices, and numerous cut-and-stained glass windows.

Fairview became both a private and public residence for Bryan, seeing it as a "Monticello of the West" as he hosted public receptions, political rallies, and lawn parties. The expansive front porch, subject to chilly breezes on Fairview's hilltop, was enclosed in 1908. Bryan made his third and last run for president that year and likely felt he wouldn't be making any more speeches from his porch.

Bryan's farm included more than 320 acres. He later deeded his mansion and ten acres to the Nebraska Methodist Conference for the establishment of Lincoln Methodist Hospital. The name was changed to Bryan Memorial Hospital in 1925 after Bryan's death, and Fairview became a dormitory for student nurses. In 1961, the Junior League of Lincoln and the Nebraska State Historical Society restored the home to its original appearance and opened it for tours, today available by appointment through the hospital. Unfortunately, the "fair view" is long gone with the development of the hospital grounds and the city of Lincoln surrounding the home.

Thomas R. Kimball's Burlington Station in Hastings incorporated Spanish Colonial Revival elements years before the style caught on nationally.

Hastings Burlington Station • Hastings

Located at the junction of the St. Joseph and Denver City Railroad and the Burlington line, Hastings's position as an important rail division town was assured by 1880. The time came to build a new Burlington station in 1902, and the city's status as Nebraska's third-largest rail center guaranteed a landmark depot.

Burlington contracted with Omaha architect Thomas Kimball to design the station. He had already designed its Neo-Classical station in Omaha and the Hastings station would also include elements of that style. Kimball, however, was looking for more—besides the Classicism in the formal composition of the building, he incorporated Beaux-Arts styling in the central pavilion and Spanish Colonial Revival in window grills, roof, and portico, and pueblo-style bracket capitals. It was in the latter that the architect was attempting to create a new idiom—the Spanish Colonial Revival would rise to prominence, but Kimball was implementing it fifteen to twenty years before that time with the Hastings station.

The Hastings Burlington Station was renovated in 1966 and again in 2000. Commercial business now takes up most of the depot's floor space, although Amtrak service continues to provide passenger rail service through the station. It continues as an important Hastings landmark and as one of the earliest examples of Spanish Colonial Revival architecture.

St. John's German Evangelical Lutheran Church and its Gothic Revival style is one of the finest and least-altered frame churches in Nebraska.

St. John's German Evangelical Lutheran Church • Lyons

Immigration to the Lyons area began in the early 1870s, when German immigrants who had first settled in Eitzen, Minnesota, moved there; the St. John's Lutheran congregation was formed in 1874, calling its first permanent pastor in 1878. A parsonage was built before a church and its kitchen served as the local school.

The St. John's congregation built their first church in 1891, but it was destroyed by fire ten years later. In 1902, they built a second church nearly identical to the first, but with a ninety-foot rather than a seventy-five-foot steeple. A new parsonage was built next to the country church in 1905. Services were held in German until 1918, when anti-German sentiment during World War I led to a conversion to English.

St. John's German Evangelical Lutheran Church is an excellent example of a German folk version of the Gothic Revival style. Unique in its rich wood and metal detailing, St. John's is one of the finest and least altered frame churches in Nebraska. The church was designed by a German-born architect, J. P. Guth of Omaha. Little is known about Guth other than, according to the *Omaha Daily Bee*, "By reason of his experience and practical knowledge his services are much in demand."

Joslyn Castle • Omaha

The prosperity of the 1890s manifested itself in the 1900s through some of the mansions built in Nebraska; in Omaha, there was none grander than the home of George and Sarah Joslyn. Hiring the well-known Omaha architect John McDonald, the paper wholesaler/newspaper magnate commissioned the construction of a three-story Medieval Scotch Baronial–style "castle" on his five-and-a-half-acre estate to create the epitome of Victorian elegance.

Officially named Lynhurst but better known as the Joslyn Castle, the Medieval Scotch Baronial–style mansion is an Omaha treasure.

McDonald made an inspection tour of mansions in Bar Harbor, Maine, and Newport, Rhode Island, for his inspiration. Silverdale limestone from the Joslyns' native state of Vermont was used to build the mansion and carriage house, hauled to the site in huge slabs that were there cut and shaped. Little expense was spared for the interior, from its 1,800-pound wrought-iron front door through the mosaic vestibule and under a mother-of-pearl ceiling. Spanish mahogany, walnut, oak, and bird's-eye maple are used throughout the one-and-a-half-story reception hall, with a grand Victorian staircase curving to the second story. A black-and-gold marble fireplace from the Italian Riviera completes the first impression.

Officially named Lynhurst, the new "Joslyn Castle" was completed in 1903 in an incredible eleven months at a cost of $250,000, or about $6 million in today's dollars. It encompassed thirty-five rooms, five baths, and three half-baths. A music room was added to the west side of the mansion in 1906 as the only major addition.

George Joslyn died in 1916. After Sarah Joslyn's death in 1940, the mansion became the property of the Society of Liberal Arts, which later leased and then sold it to the Omaha Public Schools for its administrative offices from 1944 to 1989. The State of Nebraska held the title for twenty years, and sold it to the Joslyn Castle Trust in 2010. The trust administers Joslyn Castle today for special events and tours of one of Omaha's most recognized architectural properties.

Arbor Lodge • Nebraska City

Unlike George Joslyn's home, J. Sterling Morton's mansion took considerably longer than eleven months to build. Morton was one of the early settlers to Nebraska City, where he built his home—named Arbor Lodge—in 1855. As his business interests grew and prospered (he was one of the first newspaper publishers in the state), Morton continued to build on to that original small frame cottage, remodeling it and enlarging it three times through 1885 to create a two-story home with an Italianate façade. He also hired Thomas R. Kimball in 1900 to build the property's carriage house.

Morton also had interests in politics—serving in the Nebraska Territorial House and as secretary of the territory—and in agriculture. A fascination with trees led to his planting rare varieties and heirloom apple trees across his estate, and he also instructed others in modern farming techniques and forestry in a tree-sparse Nebraska. He became the founder of Arbor Day and was later appointed as US Secretary of Agriculture by President Grover Cleveland. When Morton died in 1902, he left his son Joy the 160-acre Arbor Lodge estate.

Joy Morton hired Chicago architect Jarvis Hunt in 1903 and began a major expansion and renovation, converting the large house into a three-story, fifty-two-room Neo-Colonial mansion. The addition of three two-story, semicircular porticos at the east (main) entrance, and south and north ends, gave Arbor Lodge a resemblance to the White House. Morton, founder of the Morton Salt Company, made this his home for the next twenty years. In 1923, he donated the mansion and the adjacent sixty-acre arboretum to the State of Nebraska. Today's Arbor Lodge State Historical Park is owned by the Nebraska Game and Parks Commission and managed by the Arbor Day Farm.

J. Sterling Morton's Arbor Lodge went through many additions and modifications in becoming a fifty-two-room Neo-Colonial mansion.

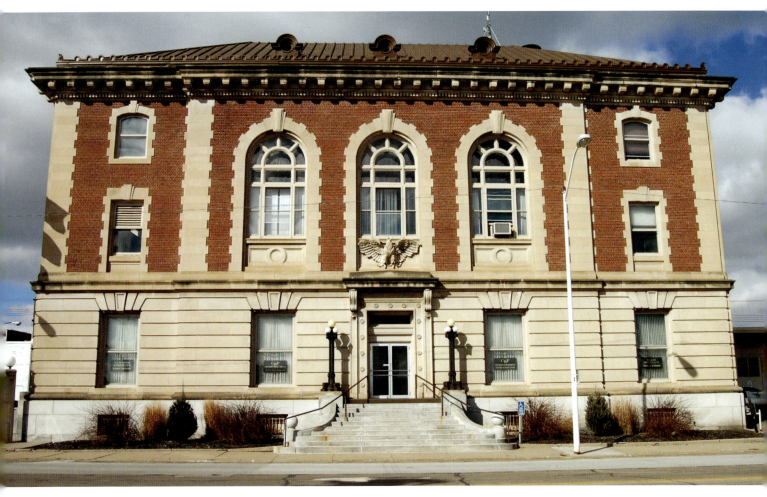

The Roman numerals for 1903 (MCMIII) led to the nickname of the "McMill" Building for the Norfolk US Post Office and Courthouse.

McMill Building • Norfolk

Congress in 1902 appropriated $100,000 for the construction of a much-needed US post office and courthouse in Norfolk, with the stipulation that the work be done within sixteen months. Working off of plans of supervising architect James Knox Taylor (essentially duplicating a government building in Annapolis, Maryland), the Congress Construction Co. of Chicago started work in June 1903 and finished in the fall of 1904. Completed in the Second Renaissance Revival style, the building was soon nicknamed "the McMill Building," due to the Roman numeral inscription of its construction year (MCMIII).

The post office made up the space of the first floor while the federal courts took the second, and a jail, marshal's quarters, and jury rooms occupied the third. In the 1930s, an addition was made to the north side which duplicated and doubled the size of the structure. The post office moved to a new building in 1970, with other federal agencies taking the space through 1974. Private developers converted the building to office space in 1976, although the Norfolk City Council held meetings there through the early 1990s. Now formally named the McMill Building, it continues as a privately held office building.

The building's Renaissance sense is shown in the granite wall surface and pressed brick trim. Few alterations have been made to the exterior, mostly through a loading dock and additional approaches. Although the interior was changed greatly through the conversion from original purposes to present office space, the McMill Building still holds much of its marble, polished oak, and tile.

Starke Round Barn • Red Cloud

The Starke Round Barn near Red Cloud is the state's largest such barn and one of the largest in the nation.

Four Starke brothers—Conrad, Ernest, Bill, and Chris—built the structure in 1902–03 after coming to Nebraska from Milwaukee at the request of their grandfather. They may have overbuilt—the building is 130 feet in diameter

The Starke Round Barn is one America's largest such structures.

and three stories tall for a total space of 40,000 cubic feet. The cost was $25,000, an unheard-of amount for any farm structure at the time. Supposedly the cost had something to do with the farm being put up for auction on the Webster County Courthouse steps in 1930.

The barn is built in three levels, with the lower for animals, the second for machinery, and the loft for hay. It's not known where the Starke brothers were inspired for the build, as this is a true round barn—most other "rounds" are actually polyhedrons of many sides. The construction uses balloon framing and heavy timber supports. The twelve-by-twelve-inch timbers are actually held together by compressive and balancing tensile forces rather than by nails or pegs.

Although on an active farm, the barn is no longer in operation itself. It is open to the general public as a small museum of its agricultural past and to the barn itself.

Hall County Courthouse • Grand Island

Thomas Kimball had a number of other projects in Nebraska when he decided to take on the design of the Hall County Courthouse in Grand Island. Kimball beat out a number of prominent architects for the assignment completed in 1904, a few of whom likely wanted to reflect the design of the US Capitol, then a popular move.

The Hall County Courthouse is one of the Midwest's best examples of the Beaux-Arts Classicism style.

Kimball instead drew upon his studies of the French Ecole des Beaux-Arts and created one of the few examples of the style in Nebraska and one of the finest examples in the Midwest. In doing so, he created a public building similar to the New York Public Library and that city's Grand Central Station, and although on a much smaller scale, the courthouse compares favorably with both.

Symbolic of the Beaux-Arts Classicism style, the brick-and-stone building includes Classical architectural detailing, a grand entrance and staircase, arched doors, pedimented windows, and sculpture and other art. The style had hit its peak at about this point, but it did prove influential in architecture for many years to come. In its nomination to the National Register of Historic Places, the Hall County Courthouse is considered to be Kimball's greatest surviving work in the state, along with the aforementioned Omaha Public Library and the St. Cecilia Cathedral.

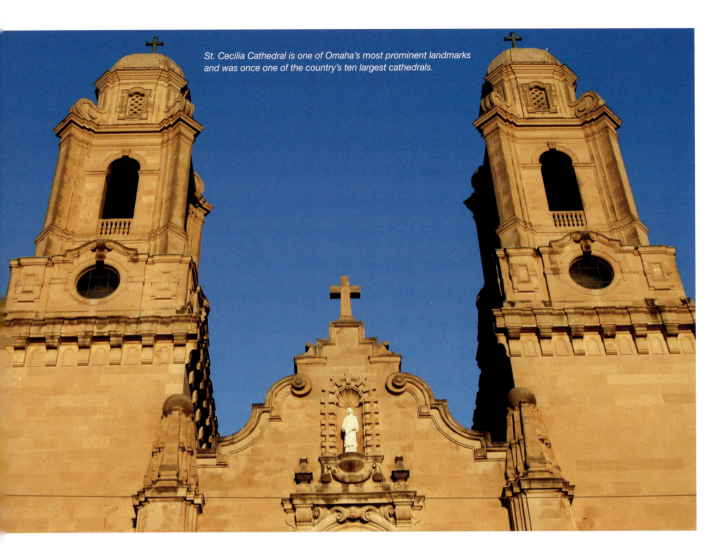

St. Cecilia Cathedral is one of Omaha's most prominent landmarks and was once one of the country's ten largest cathedrals.

St. Cecilia Cathedral • Omaha

One of the most dramatic features of the Omaha cityscape and perhaps the "magnum opus" of Nebraska's greatest architect is the glorious St. Cecilia Cathedral.

Designed by Thomas Kimball, St. Cecilia's was among the country's ten largest cathedrals when completed. Kimball was at the peak of his career with the cathedral's design and made a complete break from the common architectural designs of the day with the use of the Spanish Renaissance style of architecture when most were of European Gothic design. Kimball's explanation for the deliberate and dramatic shift to the Spanish Renaissance style drew from Nebraska history and the 1541 expedition of Coronado into the state. As Kimball explained, the first clergyman to visit the region that included Nebraska would have been a Spanish Catholic priest on the expedition. He stated that St. Cecilia's was to "be among the first, if not the first, built in the United States strictly following the Old Country conventions." Kimball's use of Spanish Renaissance preceded its national popularity as a style by at least a decade.

Visitors to Omaha almost can't miss seeing St. Cecilia's. It occupies one of the highest ridges in the city and adds another 187 feet to the 1,200-foot elevation. The twin-towered façade faces the west—perhaps not expected, as virtually all of Omaha faced the east when construction started in 1905, but Kimball clearly embraced the symbolism of addressing the western expansion of the nation and Nebraska.

For those visiting the cathedral, the size and scope are awe-inspiring. The main façade shows the rich detail found throughout the structure along with unadorned twin towers. The towers use volute curves, used throughout the building as a unifying feature. Massive buttresses flank and continue around the apse to give the building a style of "brilliant contrasts than [of] harmony," said the *Omaha Bee* in 1902.

At fifty-four years, the St. Cecilia Cathedral was the longest building project in state history, with construction beginning in 1905, services first being held in the cathedral in 1916, and completion with the finishing of the towers' domed cupolas in 1959 (at which point the cathedral was consecrated). The diocese made the decision to never go into debt over the cathedral, and construction continued as funds were available. As a result, Kimball never saw the completion of his greatest work, having died in 1934.

Chautauqua Pavilion • Hastings

Although it began at Lake Chautauqua, New York, in 1874, Nebraska soon became a leader in the Chautauqua movement. These outdoor summer events originally focused on religion in order to bring Sunday school instruction to rural communities, but as the number of attendees increased and the stay-over days increased, Chautauquas increasingly hosted musical performers and political lectures and debates as well as sermons. Nebraska's own William Jennings Bryan was considered the most popular Chautauqua speaker and rose to national prominence via these presentations.

Most of these events were held under large tents with attendees bringing tents of their own to camp out during the duration of the Chautauqua. By the turn of the new century, some communities were building permanent facilities, and among those in Nebraska was the city of Hastings. In 1907, a group of local businessmen and a congregational church formed an association to build not only a 3,500-seat pavilion but a truly remarkable, unique structure.

The octagonally oriented building solved a major engineering problem of a large space without visually blocking support columns. The support of the massive roof is gained on what might be an original approach of using large triangular trusses on exterior columns to support the Howe trusses of the pavilion. It not only works, but is attractive to the eye and exceptionally rare.

The Chautauqua movement ended by the 1920s as movie theaters and radio drew away attendees. Located in Chautauqua Park and maintained by the city, however, the Hastings pavilion continues to have use, including the hosting of modern-day Chautauquas.

Hastings's Chautauqua Pavilion is a rare example of a large space not supported by visually blocking support columns.

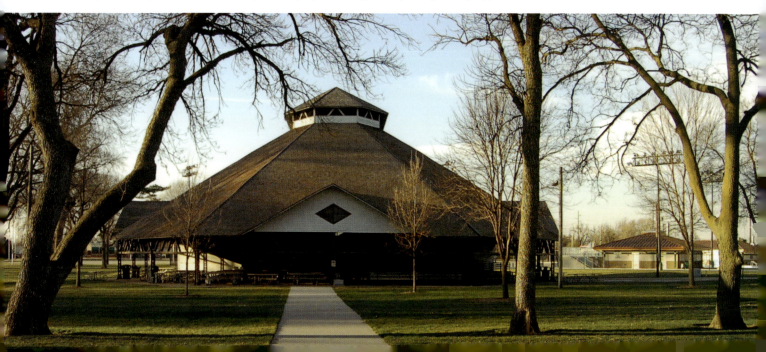

The H. P. Sutton House in McCook is Nebraska's only Frank Lloyd Wright building.

Sutton House • McCook

Around 1900, jeweler and Burlington Railroad band director Harvey Sutton and his wife Eliza wanted to enlarge their home overlooking downtown McCook. Rather than take on an informal remodeling area, the Suttons decided to hire a young architect whose work was demonstrated in the widely read *Ladies' Home Journal* in 1901. This was the first time many people had heard of Chicago architect Frank Lloyd Wright, and although many people read the article, the Suttons were the only ones to commission Wright to design a home.

Designed in 1905 and completed in 1908, the home came in the middle of Wright's first golden age, that of the Prairie Home, and is the first in a series of his career's heyday in that field. Although Mrs. Sutton repeatedly told Wright to be economical, the bid price of $5,000 was completed at double the amount and infuriated the Suttons. The home was not among the architect's best, missing many of the details that later made Wright one the country's most celebrated architects, but it did continue the overriding principles of those homes. In the Sutton home, one sees the flowing, interconnected spaces, the strong horizontal emphasis to emulate the plains, the low-pitched roofs and generous overhangs, and the horizontal strips of windows.

Unfortunately, a 1932 fire caused considerable damage to the interior of the home and destroyed the original veranda roof. The local builders were unable to determine how the roof was attached to the building and ultimately changed its location and proportions while adding large columns to support the extension. A subsequent owner, a physician, made substantial changes to the interior, cutting through oak floors, removing and covering doors, and adding walls. Later owners attempted to restore as much of the original plan as possible, retaining a Wright expert restoration architect. The home continues today as a private residence.

US Indian School • Genoa

The federal government created twenty-five US Indian Industrial Schools for the assimilation of tribal children into European-American culture by being taught to read, write, and speak English, adopt Christianity, and learn a vocation. The fourth of these schools was established in 1884 in Genoa, selected as a site due to the government owning the former Pawnee Reservation there.

The school eventually came to host nearly six hundred students, drawn from twenty tribes in ten states. Over time, nearly forty buildings were constructed on the 640-acre school grounds, providing housing for the students as well as barns for horses and dairy and beef cattle but also shops for manual skills.

The school was closed in 1934 with the students then being educated in their home communities and reservations. Most of the Genoa Indian School buildings were razed over time, including the dormitories, dining hall, and academic buildings. Of the small number of buildings that remain, the most prominent is the Manual Training Building, a two-story redbrick building constructed in 1907, with its eastern half added in 1911. The structure—with open floors on both levels—housed the blacksmith, carpentry, tailoring, and harness-making shops. Restored, the building is now the Genoa Indian School Interpretive Center, offering museum exhibits and tours.

Genoa's US Indian School Manual Training Building saw its left half built in 1907 and the right side in 1911.

Thomas Rogers Kimball: A Legacy

As Nebraska's greatest architect, Thomas Rogers Kimball left a legacy as more than just the designer of many of the state's landmark buildings.

Thomas Rodgers Kimball

Born in Cincinnati, Kimball moved to Omaha with his parents in the mid-1870s. His father Thomas Lord Kimball was vice president and general manager with the Union Pacific Railroad; the Nebraska town and county of Kimball on the Union Pacific route were named for him.

Thanks to his father's respectable position and standing, the junior Kimball could afford an education in the new degreed field of architecture. Kimball attended the University of Nebraska for two years before moving to Boston in 1880, where he studied under a private tutor and at an art school before attending the Massachusetts Institute of Technology from 1885 to 1887 as a special student in architecture. MIT offered the best architecture program in the country at the time, and it was here that he was schooled in all facets of the profession, including design theory and building fundamentals. Further development of his artistic talents came in 1887 in France, where he studied under the landscape painter Henri Harpignies.

He began a partnership with one of his MIT instructors, C. Howard Walker. As one of the few finely educated architects in the country, Kimball could have located in any city; however, while Walker practiced in Boston, Kimball and his wife of two years, Annie McPhail, moved to Omaha, where he opened the firm's branch office in 1891. Partially through his father's connections, but also through his immediately becoming active in the city's higher social circles, Kimball's first commission was for the new Omaha Public Library, an outstanding example in the City Beautiful movement.

Kimball's connections served him well. Through the design of a resort in Wyoming for railroad executives and Omaha businessmen, Kimball was assigned to design the new Burlington Station in the city. Designing the home of Omahan Gurdon Wattles—organizer of the city's Trans-Mississippi and International Exposition (1898)—led to the assignment (and national praise) of the firm of Walker & Kimball as Architects-in-Chief of the expo.

Walker & Kimball mutually separated on friendly terms after the Trans-Mississippi, and the latter began to stretch his talents and his capacity, taking on private residences and public buildings, such as the F. P. Kirkendall House in Omaha, the University of Nebraska Administration Building in Lincoln, and the Hall County Courthouse in Grand Island. Libraries, warehouses, schools, churches, office buildings, hotels, banks, carriage houses, and more were all part of his repertoire in a career of more than fifty years.

Kimball had a remarkable foresight for style. The Classical style for rail stations came into national prominence by 1900, but he established it nearly a decade earlier for the Omaha Burlington Station. He developed a Spanish Colonial Revival style for the St. Cecilia Cathedral and the Hastings Burlington Station, nearly two decades before the design became a popular standard. As former partner William Steele once stated, Kimball "did not . . . as the majority of his contemporaries did, absorb a repertoire of French tricks and come home. He studied architecture as *building*, not as merely drawings of the buildings. He seemed to have acquired at an early age that grasp of fundamental principles which was to keep him from being stampeded by passing fads."

One of Kimball's first Nebraska projects was the 1894 Nebraska Telephone Company building in Lincoln.

It can't be questioned that Kimball had an effect on the architects with whom he worked and who worked for him. A number of those associates and their projects went on to success and recognition for themselves—in this limited book alone, Kimball's partners, employees, and protégés include George B. Prinz, Clarence Wiggington, William Steele, Jacob Nachtigall, and Hershel Elarth.

He acted as an advocate for good architecture. Theodore Roosevelt appointed Kimball to the first Commission for Fine Arts, and he was assigned to many committees of the national American Institute of Architects. He was twice elected as president of the AIA, reflecting the national respect in which he was held by his peers.

Kimball had a tremendous impact on the architectural heritage of Nebraska, but his greatest influence is perhaps felt through a project he didn't design—the Nebraska State Capitol. With his selection as consultant to the capitol commission, Kimball wrote the rules to ensure submitted designs couldn't be judged on the name of the architect, nor could the architect design for known judges. His double-blind competition ensured fairness, creativity, and excellence and established standards still used today by the AIA in competitions.

One of Kimball's last projects in Nebraska was the Federal Office Building in Omaha, completed seven months before his death in 1934.

The winning architect, Bertram Goodhue, later gave credit to Kimball's judging process for freeing him to create his radically creative but highly functional design still admired today. Goodhue's premature death in 1924 before the capitol's completion continued Kimball's strong involvement in the project, with Harry Francis Cunningham as lead architect during the tower phase of construction. (Cunningham went on to establish the first school of architecture at the University of Nebraska.)

Kimball's encouragement that all submitting firms in the competition provide a comprehensive, collaborative team—for landscaping, art, and iconography of the building—was an innovative move that is expected today in such projects.

In the course of his career, Kimball left a record of quantity in addition to quality—his job book logged 871 commissions with 167 new residential buildings and 162 new non-residential structures. For all of his personal and professional success, however, Kimball found misfortune at the end of his life as one of many left destitute by the collapse of the stock market in 1929.

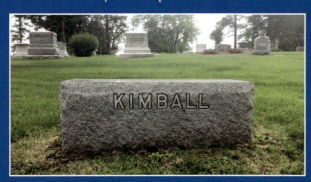

Kimball died on September 7, 1934, at the age of seventy-two. He is buried in Omaha's Forest Lawn Cemetery under a block of smooth- and rough-cut granite, bearing only his last name in block letters. On August 2, 2017, Kimball was named as the next inductee of the Nebraska Hall of Fame.

One-time Kimball draftsman Jacob Nachtigall was the designer of the St. Bonaventure Catholic Church at Raeville, one of several churches designed by the architect.

Laying the Track

The 1910s

The railroads continued their expansion across Nebraska during the 1910s, with tracks furthering their reach into more distant communities but also with the construction of new depots. Grand Island, Holdrege, and Nebraska City each saw new passenger stations from the Burlington Railroad, and Fairbury received a depot and warehouse from the Rock Island Line.

Courthouses continued to be built in Nebraska in the decade, usually to replace the counties' first efforts at the structures. Unlike the 1880s and '90s, however, these courthouses weren't as ostentatious. There were columned entrances (such as found at Burt, Clay, Custer, Douglas, and Pawnee counties), but gone were the massive central towers and domed corners of previous years. It was quite often a function of budget, but smaller counties like Hooker and Keya Paha all but dispensed with the ornamentation of their courthouses to emphasize simple functionality.

The estate of industrialist Andrew Carnegie continued to fund the construction and inventory of new libraries across the nation and in Nebraska. A total of sixty-nine Carnegie libraries were built in Nebraska from 1899 to 1917, many of which still stand and serve their communities. By far, the 1910s saw the most construction of the libraries in Nebraska with forty-six.

Nebraskans also found more venues for their entertainment. Opera houses were built for towns like Clarkson, Diller, and Lodgepole; theaters came to Rushville, Broken Bow, and Central City; and the spectacular Orpheum Theater was built in Omaha.

There was also suffering in Nebraska, particularly on some of the state's Indian reservations. The nation's first female Native American physician returned to her home in Nebraska to treat her people and build a landmark hospital.

Thomas Kimball had left his mark on the Nebraska landscape and continued to do so, but now those who had learned under his employment were striking out and making their impression in 1910s architecture.

The 1910s saw the outbreak of world war in Europe in 1914, but the official US policy of neutrality kept the war from impacting Nebraska. Once America entered the war in 1917, an anti-German feeling swept over the state. German-language newspapers, school instruction, and even religious services were all fought. Still, the German settlers in Nebraska persisted and continued to embrace their culture, seeing the construction of the Deutsche Evangelisch Lutherische Zion Kirche in Staplehurst in 1918.

The Evans House incorporates elements of four different architectural styles popular in the early 1900s.

Evans House • Columbus

Considering the prominent residents of Columbus, Dr. Carroll and Lorena Evans were among the top. Evans was a successful surgeon in the city and a general with the Nebraska National Guard, and Lorena was a niece of the famed Indian Wars scouts Frank and Luther North.

It stands to reason that when they built a new home in their town, it was a home that would make a statement. Employing local architect Charles H. Wurdeman, the Evanses in 1911 created a twenty-eight-room, 17,000-square-foot mansion incorporating elements of Renaissance, Greek, Colonial, and Spanish Revival, all popular styles in the early 1900s. All of the roofs on the mansion incorporate clay tile for the Spanish influence, the cornice work evokes the Colonial Revival, the portico and main entrance represent the Greek Revival, and its Ionic columns recall the Renaissance style. The columns were carved in the eastern United States and transported by rail; a spur was built to move the columns from the rail yard to the site.

Wurdeman's work was recognized as being the work of a master, incorporating the four principles of compositional balance, rhythm, proportion, and scale, while creating a feeling of dignity and excitement. The architect created a number of other projects in the city, including the Platte County Courthouse, Pawnee Park Stadium, schools, churches, a library, a bank, and the YMCA. After a series of private owners, the Evans House underwent a complete restoration in the first half of the 2010s and is today used as private offices.

Argo Hotel • Crofton

During the first quarter of the twentieth century, Nebraska saw a building boom in hotels. Across the state, in towns of all sizes, hotels were going up—brick, multi-floor properties with indoor plumbing and gas or electric lighting, catering to business travelers on the rail.

The Argo Hotel in Crofton was one of those modern hotels. Built in 1912 at the end of the Chicago and Northwestern rail line, the Argo served the two passenger trains arriving daily; it would eventually take in business travelers coming in from the Meridian Road, also founded in 1912.

The Argo was a commercial Prairie-style building, a popular architectural treatment of the time. It hosted a lobby, dining room, kitchen, and two bathrooms on the main floor, and twenty rooms and one bathroom on the second. The original owners sold the hotel in 1922, and subsequent owners in 1924 changed the name to the New Meridian Hotel to reflect the road's upgrade to the Meridian Highway. In 1940, the hotel was sold to become the New Meridian Sanitarium, offering hot baths and physical therapy. A local doctor made it his offices in 1962.

The building sat vacant for a number of years until a new owner restored and reopened the Argo Hotel in 1994. It now operates as a bed and breakfast in Crofton.

The Argo Hotel was one of many modern hotels which sprung up across Nebraska after the turn of the century.

Omaha (Central) High School • Omaha

When Lincoln was made the capital of Nebraska in 1867, the legislature granted the old territorial capitol and ten-acre site in Omaha to the city with the stipulation that it become a high school. Never a solid structure, the old capitol was eventually torn down and replaced by a stunning three-and-a-half-story Victorian building. That school proved to be of poor ventilation and eventually overcrowded, leading to the construction of a new Omaha High School in 1900.

Omaha architect John Latenser Sr. was hired to design the school. The Liechtenstein-born and German-educated architect had experience in school design—by the time of his death in 1936, he had designed thirty-five public schools in Omaha alone, along with others in Nebraska and western Iowa. The new Omaha High School, however, was the only one designed in the French Renaissance Revival style. The "Capitol Hill" location required a structure that was unique to the Midwest and without traditional American architecture.

The school was built in four phases over twelve years, with the east wing finished in 1901 and connected to the original school with covered hallways to eliminate the congestion. The building was completed in 1912, when the original school was also torn down to create the school's central courtyard and the north wing was finished.

Now known as Omaha Central High School, the school is a widely recognized public college-preparatory institution that has produced Nobel Prize and Academy Award winners, Medal of Honor recipients, members of Congress, sports hall of fame inductees, and leaders in academics, the arts, commerce, and industry.

John Latenser's design for the Omaha High School shunned American architectural traditions for the French Renaissance Revival style.

Architect Oscar Kirschke added elements to the Hooker County Courthouse not typically found in Nebraska.

Hooker County Courthouse • Mullen

The courthouse in Hooker County in large part owes its existence to a federal act to encourage Sand Hills settlement.

Located in the heart of the hills, the homestead allowance of 160 acres wasn't enough to make a go of it for cattle ranching. With the passage of the Kinkaid Act in 1904 to increase the homestead to 640 acres, the land rush increased the tax base and the need for a new courthouse to replace the wood-frame courthouse in Mullen.

The county hired Grand Island architect Oscar R. Kirschke to design their new county capitol (Kirschke is also noted for his design of the 1915 Liederkranz building in Grand Island). For Hooker County, Kirschke incorporated elements not usually found in Nebraska courthouses but which were popular in the early twentieth century. The redbrick-and-limestone building is of a single story on a raised basement, using the brick and stone for distinctive geometric features. The ornamentation is simple—above the entrance are two stone panels, inscribed as "1912" and "Hooker County." Large, Chicago-style windows with transoms at center bring ample natural light into the building. It also includes long corridors rather than a central hallway to reach its offices.

Hotel Flatiron • Omaha

Omaha banker and real estate investor Augustus F. Kountz (a founder of the First National Bank of Omaha) took on the city's downtown triangular intersection and block in 1911 to construct a four-story, three-sided building for commercial and office space. The architect was George B. Prinz, who formerly worked for Thomas R. Kimball and established his own firm two years earlier.

Prinz came up with a somewhat–Georgian Revival style with symmetrical façades and simple detailing to create one of the city's most distinctive buildings. The brown-brick structure's symmetrical face sits on the side of St. Mary's Avenue, with a slightly projecting wall surface and limestone trim. The Flatiron (named for the wedge-shaped clothes iron) gave a dramatic presence to the intersection, visible from several blocks away.

By 1914, the building was renovated for lodging as the Hotel Flatiron; during the 1920s and '30s, mobsters were supposedly using it as a safe house. The hotel operated for decades but saw a return to office space in the 1970s, with a restaurant on the main floor. In 2014, an investors group again renovated the 40,000-square-foot building, rebranding it as the Hotel Flatiron with luxury apartments on the upper floors and the Flatiron Café and commercial space at street level.

The past of Omaha's Hotel Flatiron supposedly saw use as a safe house for mobsters.

Clarence Wiggington's design was a first-place winner in a 1909 Good Housekeeping *contest for best two-family dwelling, later built as the Broomfield Rowhouse.*

Broomfield Rowhouse • Omaha

John H. "Jack" Broomfield was a former Pullman porter who came to Omaha in 1887 after he'd lost a leg in a train wreck. After a few odd jobs and owning a saloon, Broomfield was hired in 1901 by Omaha political boss Tom Dennison as one of his lieutenants and to run (with his partner Billy Crutchfield) the notorious and nationally known Midway Saloon, a drinking and gambling hall that catered mostly to African-Americans. He ran the saloon until 1917, when Nebraska's prohibition law forced its closing.

The rowhouse owned by Broomfield was built in the heart of Omaha's black community, right after the devastating Easter Sunday tornado of 1913 destroyed and damaged much of the neighborhood. Broomfield hired as his architect Clarence Wiggington, likely Omaha's only black architect and one of only fifty-nine black architects, artists, and draftmen listed in the 1910 census. Wiggington worked for Thomas R. Kimball, where he learned his skills as a draftsman. He left Kimball to start his own firm, and the Broomfield Rowhouse is one of nine he designed for some of the leaders of the African-American community.

A nearly identical rowhouse—the Crutchfield—once stood next to the Broomfield. Both were of the commercial form with Craftsman detailing. The Broomfield has had a renovation, although the original wood windows were replaced with aluminum.

The Picotte Hospital's Craftsman design was by future Thomas Kimball partner William Steele.

Picotte Memorial Hospital • Walthill

Susan LaFlesche Picotte holds the distinction of being the nation's first female Native American physician. Born in 1865 on the Omaha Reservation as the daughter of Omaha Indian chief Joseph LaFlesche and granddaughter of the first Army physician in Nebraska, "Dr. Sue" chose to return to her northeastern Nebraska reservation after her training to administer medical care to both her people and the whites of the area. She was an active supporter of the temperance movement after her husband Henry Picotte died of alcoholism in 1905 and a leading voice in the government's eventual ban of alcohol sales on reservations.

Picotte always worked to improve healthcare on the reservation and successfully fought for the construction of a hospital in Walthill in 1913; in its first year, it treated almost 450 people, including 126 Indians. The doctor barely enjoyed its success, however, dying in 1915 at the age of fifty from what is thought to have been bone cancer, a painful condition for about half of her life. The Walthill Hospital was renamed as the Susan Picotte Memorial Hospital in her honor.

The one-and-a-half-story Craftsman-style building was designed by Sioux City architect William Steele (who later partnered with Thomas Kimball) and was built on a hill to the northwest of Walthill. It continued to serve the community through the late 1940s, and after its closing the structure was used as a nursing home, bakery, family home, and auto upholstery business. Today it is a museum with exhibits on the history of church missions, the Omaha and Winnebago tribes, and Susan Picotte.

West Lawn Mausoleum • Omaha

The West Lawn Mausoleum of West Lawn Cemetery in Omaha is a structure of considerable rarity, both for its size and for the man who designed it.

The 1913 mausoleum is the work of master architect Henry Bacon, best known as the designer of the Lincoln Memorial in Washington, DC. It is the only Bacon-designed building in Nebraska, although he also designed the base of the Daniel Chester French sculpture at the west entrance of the Nebraska State Capitol and the base of French's sculpture in the Lincoln Memorial.

Like his Lincoln Memorial design, Henry Bacon's West Lawn Mausoleum shows the architect's favor for the Greek Revival Style.

Bacon made a specialty out of designing settings for memorials and monuments. He designed several mausoleums for wealthy individuals and families, but the West Lawn structure is apparently the only "community" mausoleum completed by the architect. Mausoleums are unusual enough in Nebraska, but to have such a large memorial for the masses (roughly 85 by 150 feet), one typically would have to go to a much larger city.

Like the Lincoln Memorial, the West Lawn Mausoleum shows Bacon's strong affinity for the Greek Revival style. He likely was delighted by the high hilltop that allowed an acropolis-like site overlooking the city. It is richly decorated and detailed and Bacon used marble extensively in the building, from the solid Colorado-Yule foundation blocks through the white marble tile floors and the four-inch-thick solid white gold-veined marble walls usually found with mausoleums.

ZCBJ Opera House •
Clarkson

Many ethnic peoples immigrated to Nebraska in its early state history with the availability of land through the Homestead Act, but probably none more prolific than the Czechs. Between 1856 and World War II, an estimated 50,000 came to the state, making Nebraska first among states in per-capita Czech immigration.

Naturally, peoples of the same language and culture tended to bond together. Strong Czech communities were established around the state, and many of the people built ZCBJ social halls in which to meet (ZCBJ is the acronym for *Zapadni Ceska Bratrska Jednota*, which translates as "Western Czech Fraternal Association"). Seven of these halls in Nebraska are registered with the National Register of Historic Places, and among the largest surviving structures is the ZCBJ Opera House in Clarkson.

Built in 1915 from the design of an unknown architect, the building is a large, two-story redbrick with some interesting detailing of bas-relief lettering, brick belt courses, a stone wall cornice, and diamond and circle motifs. The Clarkson ZCBJ Opera House was not only a meeting place for the fraternal group but also provided a venue for many organizations and events. It was here the community could meet for Memorial Day services, political speeches, dances, and various lodge meetings, and also see the touring entertainment companies and performance acts. As those purposes waned, the hall continued for other purposes and has been maintained over its first century.

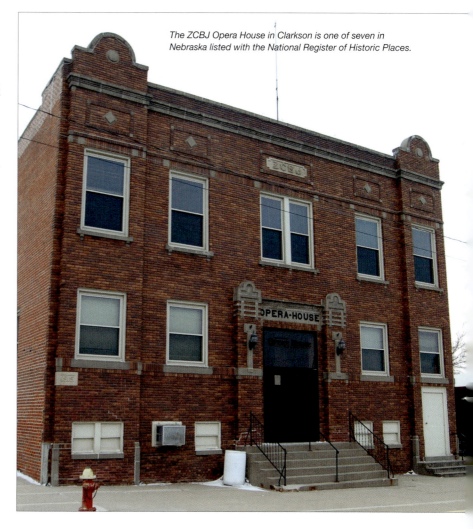

The ZCBJ Opera House in Clarkson is one of seven in Nebraska listed with the National Register of Historic Places.

One-time Kimball draftsman Jacob Nachtigall was the designer of the St. Bonaventure Catholic Church, one of several designed by the architect.

St. Bonaventure Catholic Church • Raeville

Many Nebraska towns were founded on speculation, particularly in hopes that the railroad route would come through and link their community to the rest of the world. The Boone County village of Raeville was one such community—town founders were supremely confident of it becoming a major German-Catholic center, and in 1917 they began construction of a monumental church to host them.

Omaha architect Jacob Nachtigall was hired to design the new St. Bonaventure Catholic Church. Nachtigall was a former draftsman of Thomas Kimball and likely learned enough from the master to start his own office and his own major church project. He in fact became known as the "architect of the Catholics," designing the Father Flanagan House, St. Joseph Hospital, Duchesne Academy, Immaculate Conception Church, St. James Orphanage, and Our Lady of Lourdes Church, all in Omaha.

Nachtigall created St. Bonaventure in the Romanesque Revival style, featuring massive articulated wall structures, round arches, and powerful vaults. It was designed to seat six hundred. Unfortunately, the railroad didn't come to Raeville; the village's population topped out with one hundred people in 1960 and today is listed at twenty-one.

Museum of Nebraska Art (US Post Office) • Kearney

The 1911 US Post Office at Kearney was another design from James Knox Taylor, supervising architect of the Department of the Treasury. During his term from 1897 to 1912, hundreds of federal buildings were constructed throughout the United States (including the Norfolk "McMill Building" Post Office finished in 1904). For Kearney, Taylor used a simplified Neo-Classical Revival design with heroic Tuscan columns and a parapet wall with balustrade openings as the main architectural features.

Many changes were made to the building over its years of operation as a post office, including replacement of the original revolving doors with modern metal-and-glass entrance doors and the removal of the built-in lobby tables and lighting fixtures. A major addition was made in the 1950s using brick and block with no attempt to match the original structure.

In 1976, the Nebraska Art Collection began with thirty pieces of art and was established in 1979 by the Nebraska legislature as the official collection of the state. The collection had grown large enough in its first ten years that in 1986 a locally initiated effort purchased and renovated the now-vacated post office building to open it as the Museum of Nebraska Art. Additional funding by 1993 allowed the building additional renovation and enlargement, including the rehabilitation of the brick-and-block addition to match the 1911 exterior.

The former US Post Office (today's Museum of Nebraska Art) at Kearney is a Neo-Classical Revival building.

St. Mary's Cathedral in Grand Island is considered one of the finest examples of Late Gothic Revival architecture in Nebraska.

Challenging Conventions

The 1920s

As is typically the case after a great war, new ideas come to the forefront while conventional approaches are moved aside. In Nebraska, thirty-seven-year-old Samuel R. McKelvie rode a wave of change to his election as governor in 1918, proposing an overhaul and streamlining of state government. In 1922, he saw the implementation of one of his proposals that led to the state's greatest architectural contribution and probably the nation's finest work of architecture for the era.

Using a horse-drawn plow, McKelvie broke ground on a new Nebraska State Capitol to replace the 1889 capitol, which the governor called unsafe and unsanitary. McKelvie also wanted to centralize state functions under one roof, establish a memorial to the sons of Nebraska who'd lost their lives in the World War, and build a symbol of pride for all Nebraskans. For the next twelve years, a new capitol was created in a style unlike and unsurpassed by any other in the country.

Houses of worship in Nebraska also showed some clear breaks with traditional architecture. Certainly, edifices such as St. Mary's Cathedral in Grand Island continued in the established form with its Late Gothic architecture, but other congregations embraced the unexpected. St. John African Methodist Episcopal Church, the state's oldest black congregation, built in the Modernistic Prairie style for its new church. The Temple of Congregation B'Nai Jeshuran, lacking a Hebrew architecture, created a temple of Byzantine and Moorish influence, while the Pilgrim Holiness Church in Nebraska's Sand Hills actually built its house of straw.

Mechanization completely changed the life of Nebraskans and directly and indirectly impacted their architecture. Tractors eased life on the farm, swiftly eliminating the need for horses as well as, to a large extent, farm hands, and the automobile freed rural people from the restrictions of distance. For example, instead of relying on the rails to move their livestock to market, feeders could now use trucks to haul their livestock to market. The massive Livestock Exchange Building in Omaha—the first $1 million building in the state—was a direct result of that mobility and success.

The automobile also allowed rural residents to travel to town as desired for shopping, business, and even entertainment. Many larger communities built movie theaters, putting small-town opera houses out of business. Cities built performance palaces such as the Riviera in Omaha for the traveling vaudeville shows, later to host motion pictures. Smaller venues also found a home for live entertainment, including the Dreamland Ballroom at the Jewell Building that hosted a new type of music called "Jazz."

Governmental entities found budgets to invest more in the appearance of their structures. The City of Lincoln used architectural design to create a power and waterworks plant attractive enough to be located on a major street. Counties such as Sherman and Lincoln also reinvested in their county capitols. Sherman County's unconventionality was in hiring an engineering firm to design their building, while Lincoln County's was in the length and cost of its construction (due mostly to corruption in the county).

The congregation of St. John African Methodist Episcopal Church showed considerable progressivism in architecture in accepting the Prairie style from architect Frederick S. Stott.

St. John African Methodist Episcopal Church • Omaha

One of the oldest congregations in Nebraska and the oldest black congregation in the state is Omaha's St. John African Methodist Episcopal Church. Founded with five members in 1865 (two years before Nebraska statehood), the congregation met at private homes and in several downtown locations before building a church at 18th and Webster in 1867. Membership continued to grow, leading to the purchase of a lot at 22nd and Willis for a new church in 1921.

Omaha architect Frederick S. Stott designed the church in the Prairie style, which is considered somewhat progressive for the congregation, given that Colonial or late Gothic Revival styles dominated church design in this era. Stott was a native of St. Paul, Minnesota, where he had his internship and his first practice in architecture. He ended up with the Construction Division of the US Army in Omaha and ultimately spent the rest of his career here, designing several of the city's public schools in addition to St. John AME Church.

Following their financial constraints, the membership completed the church on a "pay-as-you-go" basis. Services were held in the finished basement when it was completed in 1923, and then moved up to the auditorium extension in 1947 when it was finished. Auxiliary rooms were completed in 1956.

"A" Street Power and Water Station • Lincoln

Lincoln's "A" Street Power and Water Station is a fascinating diversion from what is typically found in a utilities plant.

The city's voters in 1919 and 1920 approved bond issues for water system and municipal lighting improvements. In building a new municipal electric plant to pump water and light streets, the city also sought much greater capacity from the plant. This was to be a structure of considerable size for the times, and on a busy street where it would be visible to many.

The Lincoln City Council in 1921 hired the architectural firm of Fiske and Meginnis, a local partnership especially active in schools and municipal architecture. For the "A" Street station, the firm developed an industrial building designed in the Neo-Classical Revival style which was a true break from the staid, lackluster look typically assigned to such projects. The building's redbrick with limestone and buff-brick trim appealed to the eye, along with the large, metal-frame windows dominating the primary and rear façades.

The new plant increased Lincoln's electrical capacity by thirty-six times and allowed for the capital city's rapid growth from 44,000 citizens in 1910 to 76,000 by 1930. Lincoln eventually turned to Ashland as the site for its water pumping station; with the original equipment removed from the building, the old "A" Street station was converted for use as condominiums.

The highly visible location of the "A" Street Power and Water Station led to a Neo-Classical Revival style, unusual for an industrial building.

Sherman County Courthouse • Loup City

Sherman County was organized in 1873 with Loup City selected as the county seat with a brick courthouse built the following year. That building, however, was destroyed by fire the day after its completion and was rebuilt in 1878.

By 1914, county residents wanted to replace their deteriorating building. When the county board failed to act, they successfully circulated a petition for a bond to build a new one. The county board met with a number of architects and in 1920 awarded the contract for a new courthouse to the three-year-old Henningson Engineering Company of Omaha, perhaps the only instance in which an engineering firm was hired to design a Nebraska courthouse. Henningson grew into the Omaha-based HDR architecture and engineering firm, observing its centennial in 2017.

Henningson designed the Property-type "County Citadel" with Beaux-Arts influences, with the standard rectangular shape, centered entrance, costly materials, and distinctive ornamentation. The use of terra-cotta for the ornamentation is considered distinctive and unusual, and above the county's name at the entrance is carved a line from Abraham Lincoln's Gettysburg Address: "That government of the people, by the people, for the people, shall not perish from the Earth."

The Sherman County Courthouse is noted as the site of the 1934 Flag Day Riot in which Ella Reeve "Mother" Bloor and other American communist demonstrators were arrested while attempting to organize farmers and workers.

The Sherman County Courthouse's terra-cotta for the ornamentation is considered distinctive and unusual for a county government building.

Jewell Building • Omaha

Omaha industries saw rapid growth during World War I, which led African-Americans to migrate to the city for its ready jobs. Most settled in the Near North Side for affordable housing, leading many businesses to locate there to serve the market. Among them was prominent black businessman James C. Jewell Sr., who commissioned the construction of a two-story commercial building at 24th and Grant.

The building was designed by Frederick A. Henninger, one of Omaha's more prolific architects, in the Georgian Revival style. The first floor of the 1923 Jewell Building would be used for his barbershop and billiards hall and two apartments, one of which was occupied by Jewell and his son, James Jr. The second floor was the Dreamland Ballroom, opening its doors just in time for the Jazz Age. It was here that nationally known acts like Louis Armstrong, Count Basie, Ella Fitzgerald, Duke Ellington, and Dizzy Gillespie performed from the 1920s through the '60s. The building also served as a community social and meeting hall.

After the building had closed and fallen into disrepair by the 1980s, it was sold to the Omaha Economic Development Corporation for rehabilitation. The Jewell Building stands today as a landmark to Omaha's musical, social, and black heritage.

One of the landmark buildings of the Jazz Age was the Dreamland Ballroom, occupying the second floor of Omaha's Jewell Building.

The Elms was the home and studio of Nebraska author Bess Streeter Aldrich during her writing career.

The Elms • Elmwood

Bess Streeter was an Iowa native and teacher with a writing hobby; during her six-year teaching career, she had submitted many children's stories to magazines, and also sold an adult story. While teaching in Marshalltown, Iowa, she met and married an attorney, Captain Charles S. Aldrich, in 1907. They moved to Elmwood in 1909 after he and a brother-in-law bought a bank, and it was here that he followed a legal and banking career. In 1922, they built their two-story Prairie-style home—nicknamed "The Elms"—on a lot overlooking the town park.

With Charles's unexpected death in 1925, Bess (with four children) was forced to turn her hobby into a profession. She had continued to write short stories for women's magazines during her marriage but now turned to novel writing. Her first, *The Rim of the Prairie*, drew upon her and her parents' experiences in the late nineteenth and early twentieth centuries, a theme she often returned to in what became a successful and acclaimed career.

The Elms was Bess Streeter Aldrich's home and her studio and is open by appointment for tours. Since her time here the gray stucco of the second floor has been covered by siding, the entrance portico has been screened in, and the wood-shingled roof now has asphalt shingles.

Byzantine and Moorish elements were incorporated in the design of Lincoln's Temple of Congregation B'Nai Jeshuran.

Temple of Congregation B'Nai Jeshuran • Lincoln

When Lincoln was designated as the state capital, the legislature encouraged the establishment of many denominations in the city with the donation of land for establishing houses of worship. Congregation B'Nai Jeshuran took two lots at 12th and D in 1885 to build a Jewish temple that didn't attract many attendees. When a fire damaged the temple, the congregation decided to start over with a new home at 20th and South streets.

Finished in 1924, the new temple, designed by the Lincoln architectural firm of Davis and Wilson, didn't have much to draw from in Hebraic architecture. Using the style of Eclecticism, their design incorporates elements of Byzantine, with the use of arches and decorations, and of Moorish, with the octagonal dome over a square hall.

The focal point of the east entrance is the large Star of David stained glass above the three arched doors. The face of the building is rich in terra-cotta trim, with flowers, plants, geometric shapes, and curved lines in the archways and the two Tablets of the Law at the gable peak. The most prominent feature is the octagonal dome with a clay tile roof rising above the roofline.

The temple is informally known today as the South Street Temple and continues to hold services.

Lincoln County Courthouse • North Platte

Probably Nebraska's most productive courthouse designer was German-born and Lincoln-based architect George A. Berlinghof. During his practice in the capital city, in partnership with Ellery Davis, Berlinghof designed eight County Capitols in Nebraska, or nearly a tenth of the state's and all in the National Register. Among them—best representing the evolution of his design skills—is the Lincoln County Courthouse in North Platte.

Like most of his courthouses, Berlinghof's Lincoln County is rectangular and two-storied upon a raised basement. Unlike the others, the entablatures of the east and west entrances rise much higher than the north and south façades, with the heavy use of brick and terra-cotta to define the resulting roof. The west (main) entrance continues the exuberant detail from above, past the columns to dentils, egg-and-dart patterns, and a small bust of Abraham Lincoln.

It also happened to be the most expensive in the state and with the longest construction period. County residents approved a special tax in 1919 for its construction, but for the next four years progress was slowed by the realization that money was not available. Embezzlement of construction funds by county officials was evident, and when an audit began, so too did a fire in the old courthouse where the county books were kept. The county treasurer and deputy were soon tried and convicted for forgery, embezzlement, and arson, and sent to prison. The courthouse was completed ten years after its start at a cost of $325,000, a record amount in Nebraska.

The Lincoln County Courthouse in North Platte was the most expensive courthouse built in Nebraska, in addition to having the longest construction period.

Originally known as the Riviera, followed by the Paramount and the Astro, today's Rose Theater continues to impress with its Moorish, Classical, Romanesque, and Corinthian stylings.

Riviera/Astro Theater • Omaha

Designed by nationally recognized Chicago architect John Eberson, the Riviera was built to be noticed. Eberson created the appearance of a dome-topped Moorish palace in downtown Omaha in 1926, yet the theater building had Classical features with Romanesque windows and Corinthian columns topped by griffons. Inside, the Riviera had all the elements of the "atmospheric" theaters popular in the 1920s, with simulated Mediterranean courtyards under a starlit evening sky.

The theater originally hosted lavish song-and-dance and vaudeville shows along with movies until changing trends ended the stage shows. The Riviera was sold in 1929 to the Paramount Company, which renamed it the Paramount Theater. Almost thirty years later, they vacated their lease to Creighton University, which closed down the theater, tore out the 2,776 seats, and leased the space for a bowling alley. In 1961, the theater was remodeled and reopened as the Astro Theater for nearly two decades. The advancement of television hurt attendance for the movie house, however, along with the development of a suburban, multi-screen megaplex, and the Astro closed its doors in 1980.

Sitting vacant for years, the building was almost slated for demolition when Nebraska Furniture Mart founder Rose Blumkin bought the Astro, presented it to the Omaha Theater Company for Young People, and led a restoration for the theater. Today, the Rose Blumkin Performing Arts Center—"The Rose"—once again entertains.

The Pilgrim Holiness Church in Arthur has survived for nearly ninety years with its baled-straw construction.

Pilgrim Holiness Church • Arthur

Nebraskans have always drawn upon their land for affordable shelter, from log cabins to sod houses. In the western Sand Hills of Arthur County, residents in 1928 built a church of straw.

Unlike many of the homesteader lands, there were virtually no trees here, and the sandiness of the soil made sod as a building medium impossible. Baled straw, however, proved sturdy and stackable and—with the right construction—would last indefinitely as a building medium. Many settlers built houses with straw and applied the same skills to build the Pilgrim Holiness Church in Arthur.

The Congregational church represents a significant example of folk architecture, using baled rye straw as a building material. Simple and practical in its design, the one-and-a-half-story rectangular building is walled by two-foot-thick bales, stuccoed on the outside, and plastered on the inside. Seven rows of pews make up the interior, while a separate room in the back served as the pastor's residence, with a stairway leading up to two sleeping rooms.

Regular services are no longer held in the building, which received a restoration in 1976. It is now a museum for the Arthur County Historical Society.

Father Flanagan's Home at Boys Town • Omaha

Father Edward J. Flanagan in 1917 created in Omaha a refuge for homeless boys. That refuge was soon moved to the west of the city and incorporated as its own community—Boys Town.

The oldest building on the campus is the 1927 home of Father Flanagan. Designed by Omaha architect Jacob M. Nachtigall in a puritanical Georgian Revival style, the house is a five-bay, central-block structure with a hipped roof and two-story wings to the south and west (rear). The west wing was added in 1940 as a dormitory for the Christian De La Salle Brothers. At that time, Flanagan ceased to use the house as his home and study, moving into the rectory at the Dowd Memorial Chapel. Flanagan died in 1948.

The 1927 Father Flanagan's Home is the oldest building on the Boys Town campus.

Various personnel lived in the home until 1974, when Boys Town officials decided to begin a restoration and make it a museum dedicated to the memory of Father Flanagan. The house is decorated and furnished as Flanagan would have in 1929, with his personal belongings on display in his bedroom and study. A desk made for him by the boys is the centerpiece of the study.

Livestock Exchange Building • Omaha

Since its founding in 1885, the Union Stockyards in South Omaha had by 1924 grown to become the second-largest in the world. The yards were on the verge of overtaking Chicago as the largest, and Everett Buckingham, president of the Union Stockyards, wanted the new Livestock Exchange Building to reflect its growth and influence.

Buckingham hired Omaha architect George Prinz—a former architect with Thomas R. Kimball—to design this "statement" building, and Prinz delivered. In 1926, the new Livestock Exchange Building opened its doors. The building was immense—this was the first $1 million project of the Peter Kiewit and Sons Construction Company, and its eleven stories loomed over the one hundred acres that made up the stockyards. Prinz designed an H-shaped structure to provide maximum natural light to its scores of offices for commission firms, banks, and other businesses. With its size, the architect also created a visually striking building of Romanesque and Italian Renaissance Revival features not typically seen in an edifice of this size.

The Union Stockyards eventually did become the largest in the world, but with decentralization in the meatpacking industry had ceased operations by 1999. The Livestock Exchange Building was restored for office space and is probably the most important existing structure relating to the stockyards and meatpacking industry in America.

The rapid growth of the Union Stockyards in Omaha led to its leadership demanding a statement of a building for its headquarters, the Livestock Exchange Building.

82   **150@150:** Nebraska's Landmark Buildings at the State's Sesquicentennial

St. Mary's Cathedral in Grand Island is considered one of the finest examples of Late Gothic Revival architecture in Nebraska.

Cathedral of the Nativity • Grand Island

Formally known as the Cathedral of the Nativity of the Blessed Virgin Mary, St. Mary's Cathedral in Grand Island is considered a physical monument to the earliest settlers of Hall County. The first settlers to the county arrived in 1859, with the first Catholic mass held in 1861 in the log house of the Reverend Anthony Moore, the county's first priest. That parish grew into the St. Mary's congregation.

The parish was raised to permanent rectorship in 1897, and in 1927, the Episcopal See of Kearney was moved to Grand Island, along with the Episcopal residence. That raised St. Mary's to cathedral status, moving the congregation to build a new cathedral.

The newly formed architectural partnership of Henry W. Brinkman and J. Stanley Hagan of Emporia, Kansas, was selected to design the new cathedral; as Brinkman and Hagan began design in 1925 and construction began in 1926, this may have been the first of many churches designed by the two.

Completed and consecrated in 1928, St. Mary's Cathedral is considered one of the finest examples of Late Gothic Revival architecture in Nebraska, particularly with its English Perpendicular Gothic tendencies. The seventy-five-foot-high fan-vaulted ceiling supported by engaged clustered columns is immediately impressionable, verticality being a main signature of the Gothic style. The Cathedral's capacity exceeds nine hundred people, making St. Mary's the largest church building in Hall County.

The Nebraska State Capitol was immediately recognized as a building of outstanding architectural distinction upon its completion in 1932.

CHAPTER 8

Depression, Drought, and Deco

The 1930s

The Stock Market Crash of 1929 had little initial effect on Nebraska, but the resulting collapse of farm commodity prices, along with a prolonged drought and "dust bowl," proved devastating for the state. Unexpectedly, the economic disaster proved to also impact Nebraska architecture.

Many of the major landmark building projects in the state began before the effects of the Great Depression took hold and were completed in the early 1930s. The Nebraska State Capitol saw its completion in 1934, and the spectacular Union Depot and Joslyn Memorial Museum were both completed three years earlier. All three of the landmark structures exhibited the influence of the architectural design called Style Moderne, later known as Art Deco.

Popularized on the coasts, Art Deco represented a complete break from traditional designs typically used by the federal government. Its projects are typically identified by flat roofs with stepped or set-back façades, an emphasis on verticality, and materials of varying colors. The details and form of the buildings are usually simple and restrained.

The style expanded rapidly with the election of Franklin D. Roosevelt as president. The new administration created numerous agencies and programs to aid in the nation's economic recovery; two of those agencies—the Public Works Administration and the Works Progress Administration—employed thousands of workers in the construction of roads, bridges, schools, post offices, courthouses, and other public buildings. Throughout Nebraska and in all states, these building projects emphasized the use of Art Deco. New auditoriums in the style were built for towns and cities like Beatrice, Fremont, Wayne, David City, Milligan, and York; seven courthouses were constructed, including those for Gosper, Rock, and Holt counties.

Omaha's 1931 Union Station was designed to express the strength, power, and masculinity of the railroad.

Union Station–Durham Museum • Omaha

Although passenger rail traffic was starting to dwindle in the late 1920s due to the advent of the automobile, railroads found it necessary to keep up appearances and provide comfort and luxury to its larger markets. The 1899 Union Station at Omaha was one of those designated for not only upgrade but replacement.

The Union Pacific hired Los Angeles "ultramodern" architect Gilbert Stanley Underwood to design the new Omaha station. The result at the 1931 opening was a stunning Art Deco design of cream-colored glazed terra-cotta and cathedral-like windows. Its exterior walls feature the sculpted figures of a brakeman, locomotive engineer, civil engineer, and railroad mechanic, which Stanley said expressed the distinctive character of the railroad of strength, power, and masculinity. Its stunning interior highlighted the windows' rose, amber, and green translucent glass, flanked by columns and wainscoting of blue-and-black Belgian marble.

The new station, along with the complete makeover of Thomas Kimball's Burlington Station across the tracks, established Omaha as one of the most important Midwest terminals. Traffic continued to decline over the years, however, and the Union Pacific closed the station in 1971 when it ended passenger service. The station today is home to the Durham Museum, named for Omaha philanthropist Charles Durham, who spearheaded a $23 million renovation and expansion of the building.

Joslyn Memorial Museum • Omaha

With the death of her husband George A. Joslyn in 1916, Sarah Joslyn was determined to create a memorial to him for the people of Omaha to perpetuate their love of music and art. She retained close friend and Omaha architect John McDonald—who had designed their home Lynhurst, also known as the Joslyn Castle—to design a museum on a site overlooking the city.

McDonald, now in partnership with his son Alan, began planning in 1920, with construction commencing in 1928. They originally planned a Beaux-Arts edifice for Joslyn. Inspired by the construction of the new state

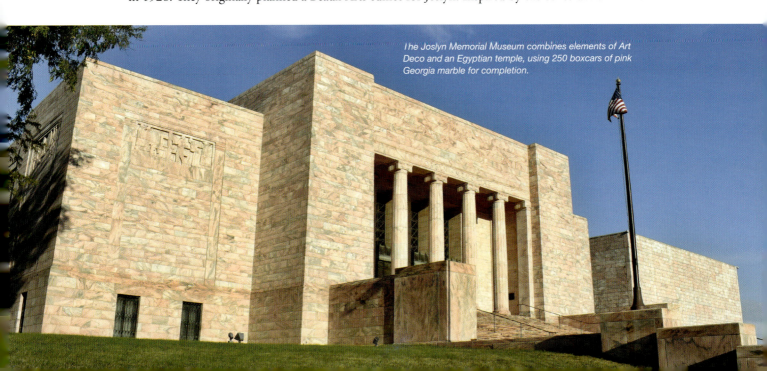

The Joslyn Memorial Museum combines elements of Art Deco and an Egyptian temple, using 250 boxcars of pink Georgia marble for completion.

capitol in Lincoln, however, they made adjustments to instead create a memorial with strong Style Moderne/ Art Deco influence, as well as that of an Egyptian temple. Thomas Kimball's influence was indirectly felt in his recommendation of a young architect, Hershel Elarth, to assist the McDonalds in design features.

The architects used 250 boxcars of pink Georgia marble for the exterior and retaining walls of the memorial, with thirty-eight marbles from around the world used in its interior. Decorative panels on the exterior were by sculptor John David Brcin with inscriptions by Hartley Burr Alexander referring to the original native inhabitants and the later explorers and settlers. This was the most expensive building construction in Omaha at that point, with final costs at nearly $3 million.

The Joslyn Memorial (later renamed the Joslyn Art Museum) was considered not only a gift to the people of Omaha, but to modern American architecture as well. A 1938 survey listed it among the one hundred finest buildings in America. In 1994, HDR and Foster + Partners designed a 58,000-square-foot addition using the same pink Georgia marble to the museum's north. The project was the first in America for Sir Norman Foster, one of Britain's most prolific and honored architects.

First-Plymouth Congregational Church •
Lincoln

In 1923, Lincoln's first and oldest church—First Congregational Church— merged with a church it had helped start in 1887, the Plymouth Congregational Church. Using the Plymouth church building initially, the united membership began planning for a new home. Plans were completed in 1929, with construction beginning the next year and seeing completion in 1931.

The new First-Plymouth Congregational Church was designed by Harold Van Buren Magonigle—best known for his memorial work, including the Liberty Memorial in Kansas City—with his associate, Robert W. McLaughlin Jr. The two incorporated the architecture of early basilica churches and Greek forums in designing the church, but also wanted to pay homage to the people and the land of Nebraska. Magonigle and McLaughlin intended for a clean break from the traditional Colonial and Gothic styles of the day.

Designed by Harold Van Buren Magonigle, the First-Plymouth Congregational Church shows some similarities with his Liberty Memorial in Kansas City.

The exterior brick walls blended six different hues of rose and gold to emulate the state's sunsets and harvests, while the 171-foot carillon tower was intended to peal across the open prairie. The approach to the church is made through a courtyard surrounded by a colonnade, to allow for outdoor activities but also encourage gathering before and after services.

The church received several additions over the years, all intended to match or complement the original style whenever possible. In 2013–2015, the Church implemented a construction project that focused on restoring the exterior of the original 1930 building and renovating the interior of the entire church.

The Nebraska State Capitol was immediately recognized as a building of outstanding architectural distinction upon its completion in 1932.

Nebraska State Capitol • Lincoln

With the legislature's approval of a new state capitol in 1919 and the appointment of a commission to oversee its creation, that board immediately named Thomas Kimball—Nebraska's most distinguished architect—as its professional advisor. Kimball crafted an elaborate procedure for a widely advertised national competition, drawing in the state's and the country's best architectural firms while hiding their identity before a jury of three distinguished American architects.

Kimball created the competition to encourage freedom of design. Emerging as the winner from the finalists was Bertram Grosvenor Goodhue of New York, who created a strikingly modern architectural style with his design of a Classical skyscraper.

Goodhue's design eliminated most of the conventional elements found in Neo-Classical capitol buildings. Gone were the columns, the cornices and pediments, the massive central dome—in their place was a gold-tiled domed tower atop a fourteen-story office tower, surrounded by a two-story base. He was one of the first architects in America to resolve the question of creating a suitable architectural vocabulary for an original native style—in this instance, a building that truly represented Nebraska, its landscape, and its people.

Although built as a memorial to the Nebraskans who lost their lives in the Great War, Goodhue integrated the themes of pioneer life in Nebraska and the evolution of constitutional law in the Western world into the building. Sculpture, mosaics, glass, furniture, murals, and other works of art thus became essential to the overall design. Architectural sculptor Lee Lawrie was retained to create the extensive sculptural program for the capitol, while University of Nebraska philosophy professor Hartley Burr Alexander planned the iconography and quotations inscribed throughout the building and Hildreth Meiere created the extensive mosaics program for the interior.

Goodhue designed an architectural wonder, not just among state capitols but among American buildings. His design came at a time of transition in architecture, however—these were the final years of Classicism and Romanticism in building design as the new emphasis was on Modernism and its clean lines and minimized ornamentation. The Nebraska capitol incorporates both; Goodhue is sometimes credited as being an early American Modernist for the Art Deco elements he incorporated into the design, although his strict adherence to art and architecture directly defies Modernism.

Nebraska did not go into debt for the construction, building on a "pay-as-you-go" basis. That meant the construction would take from 1922 to 1932 to complete and also—unfortunately—that Goodhue never saw the completion of his finest work. He died unexpectedly in 1924 at the age of fifty-four. Harry F. Cunningham took over as lead architect following Goodhue's death and subsequently established the School of Architecture at the University of Nebraska.

Barnes Oil Company • Ashland

The popularity of the automobile led to the construction of better roads and then highways to serve the traveling public. Echoing the trails of old, Nebraska gained several cross-country routes, notably Route 20, following the Niobrara River; Route 30—the Lincoln Highway—following the Platte; and Route 6, called the Omaha-Lincoln-Denver (OLD) Highway.

The former Barnes Oil Company service station (now a bank) displays an effort to help such structures blend in with their communities.

Motels, diners, and service stations were built along the highways to capture the dollars of the travelers, and the better ones employed architects to attract drivers as well as to be attractive in their communities. The Barnes brothers of Ashland, who already owned three gas stations in town, hired Lincoln architect John O. Unthank to design their fourth along Route 6. He developed a Tudor-style cottage design for the new station, opening in 1932. In fitting with the cottage type, it carried a steeply pitched roof with wood half-timbering in stuccoed gable ends. The main body of the building is dark brownish-red brick, and projecting from the main façade is the brick-piered porte cochere.

Eventually the station was closed. In 2003, the Famers and Merchants National Bank of Ashland bought the building for restoration and application for inclusion in the National Register of Historic Places, both completed for the bank by Berggren Architects of Lincoln. It is now used by the bank as a remote loan office.

Linoma Beach Lighthouse • Ashland

Not far from the Barnes Oil Company is another site that owes its existence to America's love affair with the car—although its appearance seems more in line with waterways than highways.

For as long as sand and gravel have been mined from Nebraska, small lakes have been created. Entrepreneurs have converted many of these lakes into recreation opportunities, such as Linoma Beach, developed in 1924 near Ashland by the Platte River. Linoma (named for its midpoint between Lincoln and Omaha) had a bathhouse, restaurant, picnic grounds, a dance pavilion, and even a rail stop to get thousands of people to visit the resort.

The Great Depression didn't depress business, but the owners still felt compelled to create eye-catching architecture to entice motor travelers. Elsewhere in Nebraska, whimsical roadside attractions included teepees, covered wagons, forts, and even a riverboat, but Linoma developers decided on a lighthouse overlooking their beach.

Built in 1939, the one-hundred-foot lighthouse originally featured a filling station at its base and observation decks on the second and tenth stories. It may have even had a couple of rooms available to overnight guests.

Tourism declined during World War II and afterwards. The restaurant closed and the lighthouse fell into disrepair, and there was talk of tearing down the once-popular site. A new group of investors bought the site in 2010 and have turned the resort into a members-only campground while restoring the lighthouse as an important example of roadside architecture.

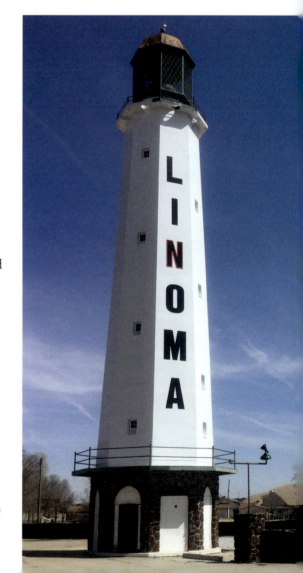

Fanciful "roadside architecture" began covering the highways of Nebraska in the 1920s, including the unusual Linoma Lighthouse at Ashland.

The 1935 Wayne Municipal Auditorium reflects a muted Art Deco styling in accordance with the lean conditions of the Great Depression.

Wayne Municipal Auditorium • Wayne

Among the government agencies created by the Roosevelt Administration to cope with the Great Depression was the Public Works Administration. The PWA was tasked with constructing large-scale public works projects such as bridges, dams, hospitals, schools, and other public structures to help revive employment and the local economy. One of those projects was the Wayne Municipal Auditorium.

Fremont architect George Grabe submitted a design reflecting the popular Art Deco style—not as highly decorated as many other buildings of the style, but more modest to reflect the lean times and the rural location. It hosts eight pilasters of decorative brickwork, four on either side of the main entrance, and between two of the pilasters on each side of the entrance is a zigzagging brick pattern. The tops of these pilasters are crowned with cast concrete caps with diamond shapes and other stylized geometric patterns.

The cost of the project was $70,000, with the PWA providing a matching grant. It took a year for the government to approve the construction, but the city found its funding with a voter-approved bond, city funds, and a donation from the local women's club. The auditorium was completed by the fall of 1935 with the first public performance—Handel's *Messiah*—in December. The auditorium continues to serve the people of Wayne.

Oak Ballroom • Schuyler

The PWA was one of the "alphabet agencies" created by the Roosevelt Administration for public projects. There was also the WPA, or Works Progress Administration, to build public buildings such as the Oak Ballroom with unskilled labor.

Built in 1935–1937 on the banks of Lost Creek at Schuyler's city park, the Oak Ballroom was designed by recognized Columbus architect Emiel Christensen. Christensen used the least expensive and most available materials: native oak from Colfax and Butler counties was used for its huge natural timbers and beams, and stones used for the foundation and walls were from the ruins of a mill destroyed by fire. The materials created a rustic treatment of the English Tudor style for the ballroom, incorporating Adirondack architectural features into the project.

The grand opening was celebrated on May 4, 1937, with Lawrence Welk and his orchestra—prior to TV stardom—performing for more than two thousand people. Covering five thousand square feet, the "Grande Dame of Midwest Ballrooms" enjoyed immediate success not only in Colfax County (Schuyler is the county seat) but as a community gathering place for Platte, Butler, and Dodge counties as well. Dances, banquets, receptions, and displays were common hosted events originally, but school proms, seminars, blood drives, and other community events were and are held here as well.

Schuyler's Oak Ballroom opened in 1937 with a performance by Lawrence Welk and his orchestra.

The Midwest Theater was an additional adaptation of the Modernistic style in Nebraska when opened in 1946.

War and Post-War
The 1940s

As could be expected, the outbreak and expansion of a second world war limited resources. Rationing was required for gasoline, tires, meat, coffee, and other goods, and shortages were experienced throughout, including labor as thousands and thousands of men and women from Nebraska were off to war.

The building boom that took place in Nebraska was due to military construction across the state, in preparation for and during World War II. A year before the attack on Pearl Harbor, the War Department began construction of the enormous Martin bomber assembly plant at Fort Crook near Bellevue. Eleven Army airfields were built across the state for the training of bomber and maintenance crews at Alliance, Ainsworth, Bruning, Fairmont, Grand Island, Harvard, Kearney, Lincoln, McCook, Scottsbluff, and Scribner. From plans generated by the War Department, the architecture was simple, utilitarian, and—for the most part—considered temporary, although many of the buildings survive today.

Works Progress Administration (WPA) projects continued around the state in the 1940s, but all agency work ended in 1943 with the low unemployment as a result of the war. When the war ended and a post-war boom began with increased farm income, Nebraska saw a rapid turnaround in new construction. The GI Bill made it possible for the thousands who served in the military to attend college in the state, and the increased enrollments meant more campus construction. Communities enjoyed new construction as well, sometimes using the Streamline variation of Art Deco, such as that used to design a new airport building in Norfolk and a movie theater in Scottsbluff.

The States Ballroom is unusual for its reinforced poured concrete construction and Modernistic, twelve-sided design.

States Ballroom • Bee

The Works Progress Administration continued to employ local men and build public projects leading into the new decade, but also allowed for completely unique concepts to be built.

The States Ballroom in Bee is one such project. Completed in 1940, the ballroom is unusual for its building medium (reinforced poured concrete) and its design and context (twelve-sided and Modernistic in a small rural community). Experimentation in architecture typically doesn't happen in a small country town, yet local architect-builder Vladimir Sobotka was fully entrusted with the project. Sobotka was not educated as an architect—at eighteen he had bought himself a building as well as architectural books to study the craft, and then took a class in Chicago in blueprint making, planning, and design. He returned to Nebraska and had designed homes, stores, schools, and an auditorium by the time he was twenty-four, not bothering to get an architecture license until he was forty-six.

The States Ballroom's twelve-sided design gave it a six-sided dance floor, which allowed participants to dance with the wood grain. It proved immediately popular with the Czech and German community of the Bee area; based on that, the town applied for and received additional WPA funding to completely finish the interior.

Plainview Band Shell • Plainview

The Plainview Band Shell is another example of the Moderne architectural style applied to a WPA project . . . at an extremely gradual pace.

The land for the park in which the band shell would be located was purchased in 1935 by the City of Plainview, which used WPA labor to level and grade the land the following year. Norfolk architect Elbert B. Watson received WPA funds in 1938 to design the band shell, and work began in June 1939. Due to other WPA projects taking place in the park, the shell's construction wasn't hurried; in fact, in July 1941—twenty-five months after it was started—the band shell still wasn't complete.

The delay was somewhat of a symptom of WPA projects winding down as the United States prepared for war, but the *Norfolk Daily News* noted that fifteen to twenty men were assigned almost exclusively to the band shell's completion for several months and would soon be finished. The town held an opening dance and "victory rally" at the band shell in July 1942, and the American Legion hosted a farewell rally and entertainment for all Pierce County inductees the following month. The Plainview Band Shell went on to host concerts, plays, and other outdoor events for generations to come.

The Plainview Band Shell took more than three years to complete.

The former Fairmont Army Airfield is now operated as a state airport by the Nebraska Department of Aeronautics.

Fairmont Army Airfield • Fairmont

With the entry of the United States into the Second World War came the necessity of flight training for pilots and aircrews of fighters and bombers. The United States Army Air Forces soon determined that Nebraska and its open spaces, cheap land, sparse population, and relatively excellent climate for flying made it ideal for training.

Twelve airfields were built in the state, including the Fairmont Army Airfield in Fillmore County. Built on more than two thousand acres of requisitioned land within only two months in 1942, the airfield was a heavy bombardment training facility. For the next two years, thousands of air crews and their support staff trained in B-24 and B-29 aircraft at Fairmont Army Airfield, seeing service in both the Pacific and in Europe.

The airfield was declared surplus after the war and offered by the government as a local airport for one dollar, but was determined to be too costly for maintenance. Most of the grounds were returned to farmland and many of the smaller buildings were sold and dismantled for scrap. Now operated as a state airport by the Nebraska Department of Aeronautics, the most prominent remaining architectural features of the site are three huge, nearly identical wood-frame hangars, sized for heavy bombers. Each is three stories high and nearly two hundred feet in length.

Lincoln Army Airfield Regimental Chapel • Lincoln

The mobilization of America for World War II necessitated the construction of training and deployment posts and airfields across the nation. Barracks, mess halls, warehouses, infirmaries, theaters, and recreation halls were built quickly for the men; religious services were expected to be held in the latter two and churches were not built.

It wasn't until pressure from First Lady Eleanor Roosevelt as a boost to the men's morale in 1941 that the military began including churches in the construction. As a result, among the 1,016 buildings constructed at the Lincoln Army Airfield was a regimental chapel. Built in May 1942 within twenty-one days, the church followed a simple Colonial Revival design from the US Army Corps of Engineers. The wood-frame building seated 362 with no decorative features, save for a four-sided belfry. It served the post through the end of the war in 1945, when the airfield was closed.

Built as part of a directive from First Lady Eleanor Roosevelt, the Lincoln Army Airfield Regimental Chapel is a rarity among World War II–era military buildings.

The City of Lincoln acquired the airfield property and the chapel in 1966. Under the administration of the Lincoln Housing Authority, the building is maintained and continues to host church services through a lease agreement. It's somewhat unusual for the chapel to have survived—buildings constructed for wartime purposes weren't built to last more than five to twenty years. That the church wasn't abandoned after its original purpose but instead was preserved at its original site and without alteration makes it a rarity among military buildings of the war.

Norden Bombsight Vault • McCook

The inauspicious Norden Bombsight Vault near McCook once held one of the nation's most secret wartime devices.

The smallest and least auspicious of Nebraska's landmark buildings was also its most secret and most highly protected.

About five miles north of McCook is the abandoned McCook Army Air Base. An access road runs parallel to the old runway and here among the deteriorating structures, within a barbed wire/wire-mesh fence, is an L-shaped concrete shed measuring eleven by thirteen feet with eight-inch-thick walls and steel doors worthy of a bank vault. This was the air base's Norden Bombsight Vault, built in 1943, and during World War II it would have been surrounded by armed guards to protect its contents.

The Norden bombsight was the Army Air Force's advanced technology. The sight was a highly accurate precision instrument used in the military's strategy of high-altitude daylight bombing, and capturing the device was the priority of the largest German spy ring in America during the war. Originally, the bombsight (when not in a bomber) was within a storage facility within five or six concrete vaults. After the bombsight was reclassified from secret to restricted, the second generation of vaults was developed for facilities like the McCook Army Air Base, where the bombsight was regularly used in bombers for training.

The base was deactivated on December 31, 1945, and is now in private ownership. The vault is now part of the display at the abandoned base as part of the McCook Army Air Base Memorial Garden.

Karl Stefan Memorial Airport Administration Building • Norfolk

In 1942, the WPA and the City of Norfolk received approval for the construction of a municipal airport at the site of a flying school three miles south of the city. Construction was delayed due to the war, but two concrete runways were laid in 1943 and the airport was dedicated in 1944.

Nebraska Congressman and Norfolk native Karl Stefan used his position on the Congressional Air Policy Board to find additional monies for the airport, including the funding of a new administration building. Local architect Elbert B. Watson designed a Streamline Moderne style, rarely applied to airport architecture. (Stefan's work also funded an office for the US Weather Bureau at the airport, equipping it with surplus Navy radar equipment for use in forecasting and making the Norfolk office one of only three with the advanced technology.)

The development of the administration building came in time for it to play a major role during the winter of 1948–49, when a blizzard shut off wide areas of Nebraska. Planes out of the Norfolk Airport delivered food and supplies to isolated citizens and dropped hay to livestock.

The administration building of the Karl Stefan Memorial Airport is a rare example of the Streamline Moderne style for airport architecture.

Changes in service subsidies resulted in the Norfolk Regional Airport's (renamed from Karl Stefan Memorial Airport) status as a general aviation facility. Its administration building now is the setting for a restaurant and bar.

Midwest Theater • Scottsbluff

When a fire destroyed the Egyptian Theater in downtown Scottsbluff in 1945, property owner William H. Ostenberg Jr. had the opportunity to build a completely new movie house as the country entered a post-war normalcy. Hiring well-known Denver architect Charles D. Strong, Ostenberg opened the new Midwest Theater on the site the following year.

Ostenberg advertised his new theater as "one of the finest in the United States," gearing it to a market that was ready for entertainment. The post-war era was the first time in more than fifteen years that entertainment was available and affordable to most. Strong opted for the most distinctive of characteristics for the Midwest Theater, embracing a Modernistic style. Audiences approaching the movie house were immediately overwhelmed by a tower entrance of sixty-eight feet with stars of pressed aluminum and flashing aluminum-cased bulbs. The interior was no less stunning, from the large screen to the blue leather and rose plush "push-back" seats. Ostenberg even bragged about the technology adopted from the recently completed war—among the materials used was Plexiglass, the material used "in the nose of a B-29 bomber."

Like most urban theaters, the Midwest saw a decline in attendance that led to its closing. In 1997, the Oregon Trail Community Foundation assumed ownership of the Midwest, overseeing its preservation. It leases the facility to the Friends of the Midwest Theater for films and other events.

The Midwest Theater was an additional adaptation of the Modernistic style in Nebraska when opened in 1946.

World War II Memorial Park • Omaha

The end of World War II and the return of servicemen and servicewomen in the conflict gave pause for the memory of those who didn't return. A letter to the editor of the *Omaha World-Herald* compelled the city's business and community leaders to discuss a fitting memorial. A site on Dodge Street (Omaha's main east-west route), near the Happy Hollow Club and the Dundee Golf Club and across from Omaha University, was selected. The Memorial Park Association was created for the collection of donations.

The memorial was one of the last projects for one of Nebraska's and the nation's great architects. Leo A. Daly of Omaha had designed numerous churches, schools, and various buildings throughout the state and nation—among his noteworthy Omaha landmarks are Rosenblatt Stadium and the master plan and most of the buildings for Boys Town.

Not all of the Memorial Park plans were realized. An amphitheater, reflecting pool, and fountain were envisioned, but not built. A semicircular colonnade at the crest of the park was erected beginning in 1945 with the names of more than nine hundred Douglas County men and women who died in the war inscribed later. President Harry S. Truman was there on June 5, 1948, for the dedication of the park.

The park has become a natural gathering point, its use ranging from demonstrations to recreation. Since 1987, an annual concert has been held on the Memorial Park grounds to celebrate America, attended by more than 50,000 every year.

The World War II Memorial Park was one of the last design projects for Omaha architect Leo A. Daly.

Mueller Tower • Lincoln

Bell towers were a tradition started in the United States after returning soldiers from World War I brought the custom home from Europe. The University of Nebraska's Mueller Tower, however, is not a traditional tower.

The university's campus last heard bells in 1925 before the University Hall was removed. Chancellor Burnett expressed his desire in 1930 for a tower with chimes, but the Great Depression put off any "dream projects" for the near future, as did World War II. The prosperity after the war, however, allowed 1898 graduate Ralph Mueller to make his desired gift of a tower.

For the tower's design, a competition was held among advanced-level architecture students at the university, supervised by department head Linus Burr Smith and selected by Mueller. The donor had hoped for a tower in the shape of an ear of corn, but George Kuska did produce a modern, almost Art Deco treatment that used a corn motif at the top of the tower that pleased Mueller.

No bells were in the tower. Instead, the new Mueller Tower incorporated electronically struck finely tuned rods of different lengths, operated from a keyboard or from plastic rolls, like a player piano. Mueller had made his fortune in electronics, and the electronic bell tower appealed to him professionally.

The university gave the design to Davis & Wilson, which had designed most of the campus buildings since 1925. When they planned to alter it to their traditional "Georgian style," Mueller objected, and the plans were given to Meginnis & Schaumberg, a Lincoln firm where Kuska was employed.

University of Nebraska architecture student George Kuska provided the Art Deco design—and corn motif—for the Mueller Tower.

Harold Eugene Wagoner of Philadelphia designed the First United Methodist Church, completed in three phases over twenty-one years.

Moving Toward Modern

The 1950s

Thousands and thousands of war veterans went to college on the GI Bill, making the 1950s an exciting time of growth, daring, and bold new ideas in American society and in architecture. The national economy—as well as the Nebraska economy—was shifting from manufacturing and agriculture to the service industry, and that was nowhere more apparent than in Omaha. The stockyards and meatpacking were on the decline, but the city's insurance businesses were on the rise, including Mutual of Omaha and Woodmen of the World, as was its telecommunication industry, led by Northwestern Bell.

Another post-war growth industry was natural gas, and among the more fast-growing and successful was the city's Northern Natural Gas. The relatively young company positioned its status with the construction its headquarters in the Modern Movement/International style, likely the first implementation of it in Nebraska, emphasizing glass, steel, and reinforced concrete.

Considered a more sparing use of Modern Movement styling is the Nebraska State Historical Society headquarters in Lincoln. Structurally the building is concrete and steel, but was intended to both complement and contrast the Nebraska State Capitol in its design. The Modern style caught on in houses of worship, such as the First United Methodist Church in Omaha, but there was also experimentation using atypical building materials, such as industrial steel panels with the Walter and Ruby Behlen House in Columbus.

As an architectural style, Art Deco had finally slipped away from the Nebraska landscape by the late 1940s, although one could occasionally see it in more rural applications, a noteworthy case being the locally designed Bassett Lodge and Café.

Bassett native Tom Galleher used the Art Moderne–style Bassett Lodge and Range Café to reflect its owner's vibrant personality and decorative tastes.

Bassett Lodge and Range Café • Bassett

The Bassett Lodge and Range Café began its life in 1926 as the Hotel Bassett, built to serve travelers to the town. The hotel eventually proved too small, as more cattle-buyers came to town for the weekly livestock auctions and the annual cattle sale. Floyd and Maude Lackaff bought the hotel in 1949 and immediately began expansion and renovation plans. They employed Tom Galleher, a Bassett native and a University of Nebraska graduate with a degree in architectural engineering.

Galleher designed the new Bassett Lodge and Range Café (construction completed in 1951) in the Art Moderne style. The building is said to reflect Maude Lackaff's vibrant personality and decorative taste—she liked modern design using glass blocks, rounded corners, and padded wainscoting. Padded, upholstered wainscoting surrounds the lower walls of the hotel, café, and reception desk, and the interior wood trim is all Philippine mahogany. Each guest room contained Art Deco–style furniture and fixtures and the bathrooms featured Art Deco–style porcelain tubs, sinks, and toilets.

The hotel has seen the booms and busts of the cattle industry since the 1950s. New owners, however, have restored the Bassett Lodge and Range Cafe to '50s Western with modern amenities while retaining all of the property's historic integrity.

Northern Natural Gas Building • Omaha

The use of natural gas as an energy source saw increasing popularity after World War II, and one of the fast-moving players in the industry in 1950 was the twenty-year-old Omaha-based Northern Natural Gas. Its rapid growth with the expansion of pipelines and customers led to its need for a new home office in which to gather its five dispersed Omaha offices.

NNG hired the well-known and prolific Omaha architectural firm of Latenser & Sons to design the new headquarters building. Latenser designed the six-story structure in the new Modern Movement style, using rectangular forms, a lack of ornamentation, curtain walls of glass, smooth wall surfaces, and open floor spaces. This style was developed and widely used in Europe, but didn't really find acceptance in the United States until after 1950; the Northern Natural Gas Building was likely the first of its kind in Nebraska.

The Northern Natural Gas Building's Modern Movement style was likely the first use of the design standard in Nebraska.

The company's growth trajectory didn't stop, and NNG found itself in need of headquarters expansion. A fifteen-story rear addition, also designed by Latenser & Sons, was incorporated into the original mass in 1957–58. Buff-colored brick kept the tower consistent and tied to the original building, but prominent stainless steel panels project forward and down to create a visual anchor between the buildings.

A 1985 merger led to the resulting headquarters leaving Omaha for Houston. The building was renovated and updated for use as apartments.

Serving as an architectural link between the state capitol and the University of Nebraska, the Nebraska State Historical Society headquarters building was designed to signify the relevance of its mission to the modern Nebraskan.

Nebraska State Historical Society • Lincoln

The Nebraska State Historical Society—the home of Nebraska history—has quite the history of finding its own home. A city block was reserved for the "State Historical and Library Association" when Lincoln was set as the state capital, but while waiting for the association to organize, the block was assigned to other purposes. The NSHS was established in 1878 and recognized as a state institution in 1883, but still had no offices; meetings and collections were held at the University of Nebraska and its library. A site was established southeast of the capitol in 1910 and plans were announced for a four-story building . . . that was never built.

It wasn't until after the Society's library was moved from the university to the capitol in 1942 that planning began for a permanent headquarters building of the Nebraska State Historical Society. A site was negotiated at 15th and R streets. Lincoln architect Ellery Lothrop Davis of Davis & Wilson was assigned the design, with construction beginning in 1951 and completed in 1953.

Davis's design incorporated the Modern Movement style, but it is sometimes complex in its simplicity. It is somewhat harsh in its horizontal/rectangular configuration, but its curved entrance block brings softness to the edges. Its lack of ornamentation was intended as another contrast to the richly decorated Nebraska State Capitol, but its shared use of Indiana limestone is a clear connection.

The Nebraska Governor's Mansion has been home to thirteen Nebraska governors since its opening.

Nebraska Governor's Mansion • Lincoln

When the legislature approved funding in the 1940s for a new Nebraska Governor's Mansion, few would have expected the debate coming from the state's architects.

Nebraskans strongly supported a new mansion to replace the 1890 mansion, seen as too small for state events and too large for one family. A committee of three noteworthy Nebraska architects—Frank Latenser and Edward J. Sessinghaus, the present and immediate past president of the Nebraska State Architects' Association, and Linus Burr Smith, head of the University of Nebraska School of Architecture—were named to select an architect. They ultimately selected Lincoln architect Selmer A. Solheim, who presented a Modified Georgian Revival featuring a two-storied columned portico.

Opinionated architects immediately spoke out, including one of the architects of the capitol, Harry F. Cunningham, who said Solheim "knows better than to place a 'pink' brick important building opposite the warm gray stone of the Capitol" and criticized the committee for coming up with a design that would "always look like a lost stray cat in the neighborhood." Some Nebraskans felt it was too "Eastern," while others said it would stand the test of time.

Despite the opposing opinions, the mansion was built and completed in 1957. In March 1958, the mansion was opened for its first public tours; over two days, an estimated 35,000 Nebraska citizens visited the new home. Thirteen Nebraska governors have lived in the Governor's Mansion since its opening.

First United Methodist Church • Omaha

One of the oldest congregations in Omaha also built one of the most striking designs for its church.

First United Methodist Church has its roots in the first sermon given in Omaha, when a Methodist from England in August 1854 conducted services for sixteen people in a log cabin. The parishioners relocated two more times over the next century until a winter fire destroyed their downtown church in 1954. They decided to relocate on a high hill on the western fringe of the city.

The church retained architect Harold Eugene Wagoner of Philadelphia, probably the most recognized designer of Protestant churches in America. Among his works are the interior of the Protestant chapel of the Air Force Academy in Colorado Springs and the National Presbyterian Church in Washington, DC.

Wagoner always followed his clients' desires, and the First United Methodist Church wanted a Modern style, accomplished over three phases between 1956 and 1977. The church was built of Tennessee quartzite stone with more than 50,000 square feet, including the main sanctuary, a smaller chapel, a music wing, a classroom wing, and administrative offices.

Harold Eugene Wagoner of Philadelphia designed the First United Methodist Church, completed in three phases over twenty-one years.

Walter and Ruby Behlen House • Columbus

When construction began on the edge of Columbus for the Behlen House, many assumed it was a commercial property rather than a residence. Few had ever seen a large flat-roofed, irregularly shaped home built of corrugated steel.

Behlen, a Columbus inventor, businessman, and manufacturer of metal buildings, wanted to demonstrate the ability of industrial products to be used for domestic purposes and decided to offer the proof through the construction of his own home in 1958. From a design by Leo A Daly, the Behlens took steel and aluminum panels primarily used in commercial, industrial, and agricultural application and built a Modernistic 8,500-square-foot single-story home.

The Behlens built the home for extensive entertaining, so the spaces are intentionally large and airy; windows in the dwelling are typically floor-to-ceiling, with a series of thirteen in the living room alone. They hosted intimate parties, but a daughter's wedding reception was also held in the house and another event hosted five hundred people. An indoor swimming pool—also built of the corrugated metal panels—could be covered for additional entertaining space. Large amounts of expensive woods were used to finish the home, including hallways paneled in Burmese teak and clear heart redwood as the garage doors.

The house continues as a private residence.

The Walter and Ruby Behlen House is a fascinating example of an architect-designed house built using industrial corrugated steel and aluminum panels.

The construction of the Woodmen Tower was seen as a turning point for the reestablishment of downtown Omaha.

Legends on the Landscape

The 1960s

The Modern Movement continued to have its impact nationally and in Nebraska during the 1960s. Two of its better-known adherents, Edward Durell Stone and Philip Johnson, were retained to make "statement" structures with the new Stuhr Museum at Grand Island and the new Sheldon Art Gallery at the University of Nebraska at Lincoln.

Another example of the movement arrived at the university campus during the 1960s with the Brutalist style and its use of raw "brutish" concrete employed for the Behlen Laboratory of Physics. The look and the building medium were almost a slap to the face of the lightness and frivolity of previous styles of architecture.

The 1960s is also when the largest office building in Nebraska for many years—the Woodmen Tower—was constructed. This, too, was a Modernistic structure with straight, clean lines, and no decorations, on a largely white block with black lines.

Still, the client and the architect would forsake contemporary architecture when they wanted. The Danish Brotherhood home office drew upon Postmodern and Late National Romantic elements while incorporating Danish detailing in numerous areas.

There was also an opportunity for experimentation in architecture. A young architecture professor by the name of Neil Astle was exploring a fascinating philosophical approach to design in several of his Nebraska projects.

Modernist architect Edward Durell Stone's design of the Stuhr Museum of the Prairie Pioneer somewhat mimics his design of the Kennedy Center and the US Embassy in India.

Stuhr Museum of the Prairie Pioneer • Grand Island

A lifelong passion for farming and pioneer history led Leo Stuhr to push for a museum to honor both. The son of pioneer farmers gave up a career as a chemist to run his family farm while also serving a term in the Nebraska legislature, as organizer and head of the Nebraska Department of Agriculture, and as presidential appointee to the Federal Farm Board.

Stuhr also helped organize the Hall County Historical Society in 1923. Before his death at age eighty-three in 1961, he offered land and money to create a museum dedicated to the prairie pioneer. Spearheading a ballot proposal before county voters in 1960, the new museum was approved on a two-to-one margin. The board decided to name the new museum for its chief benefactor and proponent.

Modernist architect Edward Durell Stone—probably the best-known architect in America—was tapped to create the new Stuhr Museum of the Prairie Pioneer. Working for the first time with his son, a landscape architect, Stone in 1967 created a white concrete structure rising from the surrounding open prairie. Although the horizontal emphasis of the museum echoes the flat land, there is a strong resemblance between it, the Kennedy Center, and another Stone project, the US Embassy in India. Stone did receive some criticism for being "formulaic" at this point in his career.

BVH Architecture completed a master plan and comprehensive renovation and restoration of the iconic building in 2014–15, at which time the museum was added to the National Register of Historic Places.

Sheldon Museum of Art • Lincoln

Funded by the estates of Frances Sheldon of Lincoln and her brother A. Bromley Sheldon of Lexington, planning for the new Sheldon Memorial Art Gallery began in 1958. The University of Nebraska's art museum had been housed for decades in Morrill Hall, the university's natural history museum, and in various temporary locations around campus.

Among those invited to submit plans was Philip Johnson, one of the nation's most recognized architects, known in the 1950s for his collaboration on the Seagram Building in New York City with Mies van der Rohe and for his iconic Glass House in New Canaan, Connecticut. Johnson's design of an elegant, contemporary adaptation of a traditional museum form was selected.

Johnson was entering his second design phase when he designed the Sheldon. He initially drew heavily on European modernism but became bored by its strict limitations. By the early 1960s, he started experimenting with incorporating Classical architecture into Modernist structures, as seen in the Sheldon. Johnson created tapered piers and arches for the museum's exterior, clad in white travertine marble cut and numbered in Italy. The interior space is centered around a two-story Great Hall with galleries to the sides, linked on the second floor by a dramatic bridge staircase. The interior walls continue the travertine, with an accented ceiling of circular panels covered in gold leaf. At the time it was built in 1963, the Sheldon was reported to be the most expensive structure ever built in the United States at $67 per square foot. The gallery was renamed the Sheldon Museum of Art in 2008.

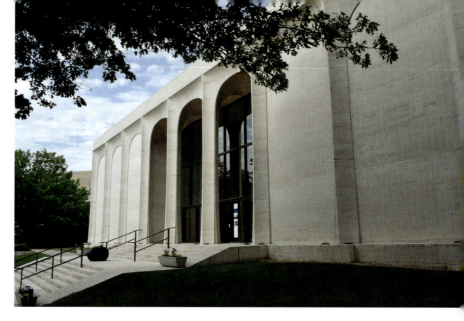

Well-known architect Philip Johnson incorporated Classical with Modernist for the Sheldon Museum of Art in Lincoln.

Behlen Laboratory of Physics • Lincoln

Brutalism was a form of architecture that showed much popularity for college and university buildings in the 1960s during their construction boom—but it was a style that didn't really catch on in Nebraska. The use of poured and precast concrete as a Modernist building medium was introduced after World War II by Le Courbusier and others was seen as a reaction to the lightness and optimism of 1930s and '40s architecture, but critics saw it as stark, oppressive, fortress-like, and "a celebration of concrete."

Still, one Brutalist building made it onto the campus of the University of Nebraska in 1965, the Behlen Laboratory of Physics. Funded by Walter Behlen, founder of Behlen Manufacturing Company of Columbus, and the National Science Foundation, the three-story laboratory contained research laboratories for nuclear and solid-state physics, theoretical physics, and x-ray diffraction research, as well as office space and a library. A 2016 renovation of the building removed most of the Brutalist features although they were retained at the roofline. It continues to serve as office and research space for the physics department.

Steele Sandham and Weinstein—a direct descendant of the firm created by Thomas R. Kimball and William Steele Sr.—was the designer of the research facility, and it's believed that architect Neil Astle may have moonlighted with the firm and completed the design. The styles produced by the firm over its nearly fifty-year lifespan reflected the tastes of the time. The Renaissance style and Art Deco were brought by Kimball to the partnership when it began in 1928, but the Old Federal Building in Omaha shows a link between historic styles and the earliest Brutalism, using both granite, limestone, and reinforced concrete.

The Behlen Laboratory of Physics was the first building to employ the Brutalist style on the University of Nebraska–Lincoln campus.

The spiral cupola and stepped dormers emulate the cultural heritage of the Danish Brotherhood national headquarters building.

Danish Brotherhood Building • Omaha

As immigrants streamed into America, numerous ethnic groups formed their own associations and fraternal organizations. This was done to offer benefits to members, but also to keep alive the culture and heritage of the Old World.

One of those groups started in Omaha in 1881 as an association of Danish veterans who had fought in the US Civil War or the Danish-Prussian War of 1864. Other societies formed in other states and a convention in Omaha in 1882 led to the founding of the Danish Brotherhood in America, with the city as its new headquarters. The Brotherhood enjoyed rapid growth for a number of years, with 283 lodges in fourteen states by 1923; its membership stood at around 21,000 members in 1925.

A call for a new national headquarters was carried out in 1966, with Omaha architect Edward J. Sessinghaus of the firm Teig & Johnson as the designer. Built on land purchased by the society in Omaha's Gold Coast/Blackstone district, Sessinghaus's design was a stylistically eclectic early Postmodern/Late National Romantic office building. To emphasize the cultural heritage of the Brotherhood, Sessinghaus added particularly Danish details to the project with a copper spiral cupola, stepped dormers, and a terra-cotta tile roof.

Under declining membership, the Danish Brotherhood was merged into the Woodmen of the World Association in 1995. The building was used as law offices until 2015 and has since been purchased for future administrative space for Dundee Bank, with AO completing the architectural work.

Flansburg Residence • Omaha

A native of Salt Lake City, Neil Astle came to Lincoln in the 1960s as a professor of architecture. Astle started his own Omaha architectural firm, Neil Astle & Associates, in 1965, and in 1978 changed the name to Astle/Ericson & Associates to reflect his partnership with architect Ronald G. Ericson.

Architect Neil Astle built this Omaha home with himself as the contractor and a mechanical subcontractor and young carpenter as the only other key participants.

Astle frequently explored new frontiers in his architecture, projects of which are found nationally, but particularly at his alma mater, the University of Utah, other Utah campuses, and in Nebraska. Some examples of his work can be found at the Mormon Trail Center in Omaha, the Benedictine Center near Schuyler (page 116), and in 1968, the Steve and Mary Flansburg home in Omaha.

Astle embraced a philosophical approach to architecture and followed modern systems theory, in which a set of elements are linked intrinsically and that a change to one element will affect the others. For this home, Astle used overlapping panels of two-by-two cedar panels, essentially "weaving" the home. He acted as his own contractor, aided only by a mechanical subcontractor and young carpenter as the only other key participants. The weaving process minimized material waste (only 2 percent, compared with the typical 20 percent), provided aesthetic consistency, and allowed a relatively low skill level for the builder with minimal tools and no scaffolding. When the three-bedroom house was sold in 1978, the new owner easily used the interlocking system to add bedrooms at both ends of the house.

Woodmen Tower • Omaha

The Woodmen Tower represented a turning point for downtown Omaha. For years, businesses had slipped away from the core of the city to the suburbs. Other insurance companies had shifted from the east to the west, opting for horizontal spaces in fields of green, and that was a real possibility for Woodmen of the World as well.

Architect Leo A. Daly Jr., however, convinced the life insurance society that it could make a statement and achieve far more visibility downtown than they would at the edge of town. Daly persuaded the Woodmen leadership to instead build a skyscraper to redefine the Omaha skyline.

The project took half of a city block, and included the demolition of the old city hall; Omaha National Bank (now part of US Bank) was signed as the primary tenant. Started in 1966 and completed in 1969, the Woodmen Tower was the tallest building in Omaha for more than thirty years until the construction of the First National Tower. The Woodmen even ended up taller than planned—the original twenty-two-floor plan got boosted to twenty-eight floors, then to twenty-nine, and ultimately thirty stories, in part due to water issues changing underground parking to additional floors and the top floor getting split to two floors (one of which was occupied by the "Top of the World" restaurant for many years).

The building's interior space has been renovated throughout, with the Woodmen of the World Insurance Society still occupying most of the 533,281 square feet. The Woodmen Tower entered the film world in 2002, with scenes from *About Schmidt*, starring Jack Nicholson, being filmed there.

The construction of the Woodmen Tower was seen as a turning point for the reestablishment of downtown Omaha.

Designed by Astle/Ericson & Associates, the St. Benedict Monastery is constructed of cast-in-place reinforced concrete and cedar wood, using energy efficiently without the sacrifice of light and view. The nearby St. Benedict Center, also designed by Astle/Ericson, includes a man-made lake as a reservoir for fire prevention.

Economy and Energy

The 1970s

Unemployment, an energy crisis, and inflation plagued the country during the 1970s, and the lack of economic growth hit Nebraska as well. The number of farms was decreasing, construction was limited, and few were the opportunities for truly unique and interesting building projects, although gems were created.

Modernism continued in Nebraska's urban settings. The National Bank of Commerce hired the firm of internationally known architect I. M. Pei to design its new bank building on a street-side downtown sliver of land and received a stunning, cast-in-place concrete structure. Omaha made its first efforts toward a downtown renewal and revitalization with the Modernist construction of the Central Park Mall (today's Gene Leahy Mall) to link the central business district to the Missouri River.

The Modernistic style continued elsewhere as well with the Strauss Performing Arts Center on the University of Nebraska–Omaha campus and the Edith Abbott Memorial Library in Grand Island. Neil Astle continued to display his use of innovative design and materials with a number of private homes, but more importantly and visibly with a striking Modernistic monastery built into the surrounding landscape for energy efficiency.

The Strauss Performing Arts Center serves as the center of musical activity for the University of Nebraska at Omaha.

Strauss Performing Arts Center • Omaha

The Willis A. and Janet S. Strauss Performing Arts Center serves as the center of musical activity of the University of Nebraska at Omaha and is home to the School of Music within the College of Communication, Fine Arts and Media.

Designed by Omaha architect Golden Zenon and completed in 1973, the complex includes a tunable recital hall with seating for 460, a Casavant organ and a Steinway Concert Grand D piano, impressive acoustic isolation, large rehearsal rooms, a listening library, and ample practice rooms for music students. Strauss hosts more than two hundred concerts, festivals, and master classes each semester.

This building is next to the focal point of the campus, a campanile (bell tower) housing a carillon of forty-seven bells.

Central Park Mall • Omaha

Designed by the Modernist landscape architecture firm of Lawrence Halprin & Associates, the 9.6-acre Central Park Mall opened in 1974 as the centerpiece for the revitalization of downtown Omaha. The public park, which covers a four-block area, links the downtown core to the Heartland of America Park and the Missouri Riverfront.

Renamed as the Gene Leahy Mall in 1992 for the mayor who oversaw its opening, the project brings design elements used in Halprin's earlier work, such as the multi-level sections of Lovejoy Plaza in Portland, and the nonlinear spine of Nicollet Mall in Minneapolis.

Pedestrians entering the mall from the west travel from street level down a series of concrete and grass terraces and pass waterfalls to reach a narrow, constructed lagoon that runs the length of the park. Sloping lawns punctuated by stands of trees and rock outcroppings make up the irregular banks of the pond, with space for a playground, gardens, amphitheater, and sculpture garden.

The mall, renovated in 2013, has become a popular event site for an annual Christmas lights ceremony and a yearly New Year's Eve fireworks celebration.

The Central Park Mall (now known as the Gene Leahy Mall) serves as the link between the downtown Omaha core and the Missouri River.

NBC/Wells Fargo Center • Lincoln

The National Bank of Commerce stood for decades at the northwest corner of 13th and O Street, but in designing the new bank for its client, the internationally known New York firm of I. M. Pei and Partners wanted to make a statement based on understatement.

The intersection is one of the most significant crossings in the capital city, with 13th as the "office building strip" and O Street as the "retail strip." The architectural team—which included the Lincoln firm of Davis, Fenton, Stange & Darling—wanted a structure that was significant in itself but without dominating the scenery. It should complement the Stuart Building across 13th, but not dwarf the smaller retail stores. Ideally, it would provide a link between the University of Nebraska campus to the north and the downtown core to the south. Although this was to be a large building, the situation was compounded by the bank occupying a sliver of a lot along 13th.

The objectives were met with the 1976 construction of the NBC Center (now the Wells Fargo Center). Cast-in-place concrete was used for the building. As James Ingo Freed of I. M. Pei and Partners said, "Everything you see is what does all the work. . . . It's a one-step operation."

Design features "nudge" people where to go once inside, such as an overhead walkway pulling people toward elevators or stairs to a basement concourse drawing people to the left rather than right. Fig trees, plants, and an earth-tone décor added a softer, feminine approach to an otherwise masculine building.

I. M. Pei's design for the NBC Center (now the Wells Fargo Center) was to link the University of Nebraska campus to the north with the downtown core to the south.

St. Benedict Monastery and St. Benedict Center • Schuyler

The roots of this secluded monastery, retreat, and conference center actually begin in pre-war Germany, when monks from the Muensterschwarzach Abbey came to the United States in the 1920s. With the rise of the Nazi Party in the 1930s, additional monks were sent to assist the growth of the mission, originally located in the town of Schuyler.

In 1979, architects Astle/Ericson & Associates designed a new St. Benedict Monastery four miles to the north of town. The new building consisted of three wings radiating from the Christ the King Chapel housing a gallery, work area, offices, commons, service functions, and living quarters.

The monastery is constructed of cast-in-place reinforced concrete and cedar wood, designed to be energy efficient without the sacrifice of light and view. It is earth-covered except for the chapel that projects above the horizontal roofline of the adjacent wings. The chapel is covered with a truncated pyramidal roof capped by a large cupola, both of which are constructed of wood.

In 1997, the St. Benedict Center was added to the north of the complex. Also designed by Astle/Ericson, the center is a nonprofit ecumenical retreat and conference center. Set in a verdant park with walking paths, Stations of the Cross, and an amphitheater, the center is built of brick and concrete with a gable roof. It features a large concourse, one hundred guest rooms, dining and kitchen facilities, a secluded library and meditation area, a large chapel, and a smaller adoration chapel.

The St. Benedict Monastery is constructed of cast-in-place reinforced concrete and cedar wood, using energy efficiently without the sacrifice of light and view.

The groundbreaking for the Edith Abbott Memorial Library employed the same spade Theodore Roosevelt used at the groundbreaking for the previous Grand Island library.

Edith Abbott Memorial Library • Grand Island

There is a rich history behind the Abbotts and the Grand Island library. Elizabeth Abbott was one of the first board members of the library, served on it for forty-eight years, and was instrumental in President Theodore Roosevelt's participation in the 1903 groundbreaking for the city's Carnegie library. Her daughters Edith and Grace were both active pioneers in American social work; Grace Abbott was the first woman to be nominated for a presidential cabinet position, and Edith Abbott left the bulk of her estate to build a new library after her death in 1957.

It was nearly twenty years before her wish was carried out, however. Plans to replace the small and aging Carnegie library were discussed in 1954, but it was more than ten years before the library board even determined that an entire city block should be used for the project, and the Abbott estate was probated. Ultimately, the library purchased the site and hired Omaha architects Stanley J. How and Associates for the design. A successful $600,000 bond issue election was held in 1972 to add to the $350,000 Abbott bequeath, a groundbreaking was held in 1973 (using the seventy-year-old spade from the Roosevelt groundbreaking), and the Edith Abbott Memorial Library was dedicated in 1974.

How's Modernistic design for the Abbott Library was chosen by the Nebraska chapter of the American Institute of Architects for its annual award in the fall of 1974.

The Peterson-Yanney Memorial Bell Tower incorporates relief sculptures from a former auditorium at the University of Nebraska at Kearney.

Building Through Recession

The 1980s and 1990s

The 1980s marked a continuation of what plagued the 1970s. The farm economy continued to worsen, while manufacturing plants experienced layoffs and closures in the state. Budget cutbacks became the norm in state government as inflation outpaced salary increases.

Again, the economic recession impacted building in Nebraska as major projects were stalled. Noteworthy exceptions were the expansion of the Mutual of Omaha headquarters building, which included the construction of an innovative below-ground dome and office expansion, and a capping of the city-end of downtown Omaha's Central Park Mall with the twin-towered Central Park Plaza.

Tax incentives to industry passed by the Nebraska legislature in 1987 gave impetus to companies to stay in Nebraska to hire employees and build; the most visible sign of that legislation was the construction of a new ConAgra headquarters campus on the Omaha riverfront. Many questioned the effectiveness of the incentives, yet the building activity was improving.

In the 1990s, many of the new architectural landmarks were geared toward education, such as the Beadle Center for Genetics on the University of Nebraska–Lincoln campus and the Weber Fine Arts Building at University of Nebraska–Omaha; others fulfilled an entertainment/leisure component, like the Lied Lodge in Nebraska City, the Lied Jungle at Omaha's Henry Doorly Zoo, the SAC Museum near Ashland, and the Great Platte River Road Archway at Kearney to close out the millennium.

The addition of an underground dome to the Mutual of Omaha headquarters created a new landmark structure without impeding the view of the existing landmark structure.

Mutual of Omaha Dome • Omaha

In desperate need of additional office space and not willing to compromise the appearance and attractiveness of its fourteen-story headquarters building, the Mutual of Omaha insurance company settled for building a landmark under the land.

Leo A Daly and Associates designed a striking underground dome for the company—at the time, the largest thermopane dome in the world. Construction was a particularly challenging task, in that the excavation went more than three stories deep adjacent to the fourteen-story tower. For that reason, the floors of the dome were progressively terraced away from the building.

The construction satisfied many of Mutual's needs: energy conservation, optimized construction costs, good use of existing land, limited impact on parking, and no impact on the aesthetics of the headquarters. In fact, the addition enhances it with its park-like appearance.

Most importantly, when completed in 1979, the dome gave the company a much-needed additional 190,000 square feet of office space for existing and future growth. The project gave Mutual of Omaha an additional three stories underground for the office space, but also provided an open and airy setting for employee dining and events. The dome itself is heated only by body heat and sunlight, and also provides psychological relief from a completely underground environment.

Milton R. Abrahams Public Library • Omaha

For this branch of the Omaha Public Library, architect Bahr, Vermeer & Haecker took an unusual approach: designing a library to not look like a library.

Libraries typically are located in residential areas. The Abrahams branch, however, is located on a major north-south retail artery, surrounded by commercial properties. The location in large part was determined by the growing northwest population during the previous decades and in its high-traffic location immediately became one of the busiest branches when opened in 1988. It was named for Omaha attorney, philanthropist, and longtime library board member Milton R. Abrahams.

BVH brought a fresh and Modernistic look to the library branch, designing a long, low, horizontal wall punctuated at its center by a glass pyramid. The skylight pyramid showcases the "Sunburst" sculpture by artist Harry Bertoia, on permanent loan from the Joslyn Art Museum.

The back wall of the library is entirely made of glass from floor to ceiling, allowing natural light to stream into the structure across the open floor.

The library underwent a $1.2-million renovation in 2011 to make the facility more user-friendly, spacious, and energy efficient, while adding better acoustics, new computers, electrical outlets, a teen room, and study rooms.

Bahr, Vermeer & Haecker's floor-to-ceiling glass wall design for the Milton Abrahams branch library allows for ample natural light.

Wick Alumni Center •
Lincoln

The Wick Alumni Center is home to the Nebraska Alumni Association offices, completed in 1985 by the New York City firm Gwathmey/Siegel & Associates, which won the project through a national competition. The three-story building is named for Milton I. Wick, a 1922 UNL graduate who donated $500,000 for the construction of the building.

The alumni center is located at the northwest corner of 16th and R Street, entered through a raised garden with a reflecting pool, trees, and seating with walls of green Vermont slate. Retaining the scale of the residential neighbor with the transition to university campus, along with the massing and siting, fully establishes the Nebraska State Historical Society headquarters as the end of Centennial Mall.

The architect conception was for an Italian-modern transformation of a Renaissance palazzo. The center's rectilinear massing is clad in dark iron-spot, Norman-size brick, with the green slate calling out the building's entry through a three-bay recess.

Two primary spaces are on an axis around a center hall: a two-story boardroom, and a three-story Great Hall. The Great Hall is a grand barrel-vaulted space with two symmetrical staircases and ample light over its mahogany paneling. The center's 30,000 square feet is layered front to back with space for offices, meeting rooms, and events, the largest of which can hold up to 450 guests.

A transitional and welcoming portal to the University of Nebraska–Lincoln campus is the purpose of the Wick Alumni Center.

The Peterson-Yanney Bell Tower incorporates relief sculptures from a former auditorium at the University of Nebraska at Kearney.

Peterson-Yanney Bell Tower • Kearney

The sixty-six-foot-tall bell tower on the University of Nebraska–Kearney campus was a gift in memory of the George and Venetia Peterson and Elias and Mary Yanney families, who immigrated to Kearney from Greece and Lebanon. Designed by Jack D. Wilkins & Associates and erected in 1986, the tower is intended as a memorial to the university's old administration building that housed the campus auditorium. The design includes relief sculptures adapted from replicas of the Parthenon sculptures in Athens, Greece, which were part of the friezes that adorned the auditorium. It is supported by four columns that stood at the entrance of the administration building.

Of course, the auditory attraction of the tower is the set of twenty-four bronze bells cast by the Paccard Bell Foundry in France. Combined, the bells weigh a total of 5,790 pounds, the smallest of which weighs forty-eight pounds and is eleven and a half inches in diameter, and the largest of which weighs 1,477 pounds with a diameter of forty-one inches.

The bells originally chimed the notes of songs produced in the 1950s, but in recent years took on more contemporary tunes from The Beatles and Bruce Springsteen and Lady Gaga to Led Zeppelin. "Pomp and Circumstance" is played during commencement ceremonies.

St. Columbkille Catholic Church • Papillion

The history of the St. Columbkille parish in the Papillion area goes back to the 1860s, when a small group of Catholic families settled in the area. Growing through two churches over the next century, the congregation was soon ready for its third.

The new St. Columbkille Catholic Church (completed in 1981) replaced the original 250-seat building with an eight-hundred-seat parish center, using warm, comfortable materials to provide a sense of community. Designed by Bahr, Vermeer & Haecker, the worship space interior materials consist of brick walls, a stained wood-beam ceiling, and a carpeted floor with the aisles covered with stone tile. Stained glass clerestory windows and a large overhead skylight shower a suspended crucifix above the altar with a warm glow. A brick tower near the front entrance houses a bronze bell reclaimed from the original building.

By taking advantage of the sloping site, the two-level brick church is accessible without stairs. The upper level contains the worship space with radial seating, adjacent chapel, choir, and cry room, plus a commons area, two sacristies, and reconciliation rooms. Two large skylights bring light into the commons area and worship space, lighting the baptismal font and altar, as well as illuminating the wood beams, wood ceiling, and brick walls. The radial seating around a central altar reinforces acoustics, sight lines, and a sense of togetherness.

By taking advantage of the sloping site, the two-level St. Columbkille Catholic Church is accessible without stairs. (BVH)

Lied Center for the Performing Arts • Lincoln

For decades, the University of Nebraska had expressed the desire for a performing arts center on the Lincoln campus. In 1933, Chancellor E. A. Burnett stated in a public address: "In time, some citizen might erect a lovely theater and auditorium for us. . . . Someday, a hall for fine arts with art galleries, music studios, and audition rooms will be built."

Several bond issues and ideas were presented to the community in the 1970s but didn't catch. Finally, after a matching grant of $10 million from the Ernst Lied Foundation Trust—named for a 1927 Nebraska alum who'd become a multimillionaire investing in Las Vegas real estate—the impetus was found to build the Lied Center for the Performing Arts in 1989.

Designed by HDR Architecture, the Center is an arts presenter, bringing to Lincoln professional Broadway productions, musicians, dance companies, theater companies, orchestras, speakers, and more from all over the world. The Center consists of five separate areas including the main stage, with 2,210 seats, the Steinhart Room, the Carson Theater, the Parker Lobby, and the Cooper Lobby.

The Lied Center for the Performing Arts design links the UNL campus to downtown Lincoln, providing national and international performances to a statewide audience. (University of Nebraska)

The George W. Beadle Center was named for Nebraska's own Nobel Prize winner.

The George W. Beadle Center for Genetics and Biomaterials Research • Lincoln

Completed in 1994, the Beadle Center is a $32 million, 140,000-square-foot facility located on the University of Nebraska's main campus. The massive structure (designed by Davis Design of Lincoln) also houses the UNL Center for Biotechnology, the Nebraska Center for Virology, the Redox Biology Center, and the UNL Plant Science Institute. Cooperative research programs between UNL and the University of Nebraska Medical Center focus on the development of new technologies and technology spin-off companies.

The center is named for a highly worthy son of Nebraska. Born in Wahoo, George W. Beadle received his bachelor's and master's degrees in science at the University of Nebraska before going on to research work and professorships at Harvard, Stanford, and the California Institute of Technology; he later became chancellor and president of the University of Chicago. In his work as a geneticist, Beadle (with Edward Lawrie Tatum) was awarded the 1958 Nobel Prize for Physiology or Medicine. He received many other national and international awards and recognition for his work, along with numerous honorary doctor of science degrees.

Lied Lodge and Conference Center • Nebraska City

Built on a wooded hillside overlooking South Table Creek, the Lied Lodge and Conference Center was constructed to encourage learning about and awareness for environmental conservation in an upscale rural getaway.

The Lied Lodge was built in 1998 from an award-winning design by Alley Poyner Macchietto Architecture as part of a master plan for the National Arbor Day Foundation and its historic Nebraska City properties. The lodge is a retreat center and able to accommodate up to four hundred people with 144 guest rooms, classrooms, conference and multipurpose rooms, and dining halls.

The design of the center is to align with the foundation's commitment to tree planting, conservation, and environmental stewardship. Ecologically responsible materials and fixtures are used throughout the center: outside, trees surround the lodge as a natural sound barrier and heat regulator; inside, un-milled timber provides the structural system, and wood from the adjacent Arbor Day Farm provides steam for the building's heating and cooling system. The lodge also has energy-efficient fireplaces, water-conserving plumbing fixtures, and an on-site recycling facility. Sustainability through high-end design is exhibited throughout the lodge, designed to act as an iconic and physical representation of the foundation's mission.

The Lied Lodge and Conference Center in Nebraska City was designed to emphasize tree planting, conservation, and environmental stewardship. (Tom Kessler Photography)

Weber Fine Arts Building •
Omaha

The Weber Fine Arts Building on the campus of the University of Nebraska–Omaha was designed as a standing invitation to explore the arts. Taking advantage of the site's sloping terrain, the facility incorporates outdoor courtyards to draw important pedestrian paths and parking areas to its major entrances.

The building combines the appearance of a medieval tower construction—with its pinnacled towers and rusticated stone walls—with avant-garde waving exterior walls, symbolizing the creativity and timelessness of the creative arts. Designed by Schemmer in association with nationally noted art facility design consultants Hardy Holzman Pfeiffer Associates, the 78,000-square-foot building incorporates the departments of art and dramatic art and includes studio spaces for painting, drawing, printmaking, papermaking, electronic imaging, art education, and graphic arts. It is also the home of the UNO Art Gallery, the Nebraska Center for Book Arts, a writers' workshop, and a 250-seat experimental theater. The adjoining amphitheater, The Castle of Perseverance, is based upon a medieval play. Separate buildings house the university's sculpture and ceramics studios.

The building opened in 1992 and was named at that time for former UNO chancellor Del Weber and his wife Lou Ann.

A medieval tower construction approach with avant-garde waving exterior walls emphasizes the creative arts for the Weber Fine Arts Building at the University of Nebraska at Omaha.

Strategic Air Command Museum • Ashland

The Strategic Air Command Museum once occupied an inactive runway of Offutt Air Force Base—the very site where this impressive collection of Cold War–era aircraft made much of its history. A multitude of factors—including base security, site accessibility, and exposure to the elements—all combined to create an innovative museum to house the craft and their history.

Opened in 1998 from a design by Leo A Daly, the Strategic Air Command Museum would seem out of place in its setting in the wooded hills overlooking the Platte River. However, its proximity to Interstate 80 and other tourism destinations created a desirable, attractive location, and the effective use of earthen berms and landscaping blends the museum into the prairie.

The facility encompasses 255,000 square feet, large enough to protect and display thirty-one aircraft, including a spectacular 14,000-square-foot glass-enclosed atrium hosting its showpiece exhibit, a suspended SR71 Blackbird. The hangar-shaped wings of the museum draw upon the collection's aviation heritage but also allow for future expansion in two directions should the need occur. An added feature is the lack of columns to support the roof, allowing unobstructed viewing of the aircraft. A two-hundred-seat theater evokes the mysterious qualities of today's stealth aircraft, providing an imaginative atmosphere for films, conferences, lectures, and seminars.

The Strategic Air Command Museum near Ashland uses the hilled landscape to blend into the surrounding prairie. (Leo A Daly)

The Bowen House was designed to give views from every room, either to the adjacent golf course or the surrounding woods. (Gary Bowen)

Bowen House • Omaha

Owned and designed by architect Gary Bowen, the two-story linear house is situated adjacent to a private golf course on the edge of Omaha. This wooded, one-acre site proved to be challenging due to a ravine running diagonally and a twenty-foot cross slope, limiting the buildable area to the west one-third of the property.

Placed on the uppermost corner of the site with the long axis parallel to the golf course, the house affords views from all rooms. In concert with the north-south slope, both the roof and the floor levels step down the hill, with every measure taken to minimize disruption to the forest setting. Disturbed areas have been allowed to revert back to the original native vegetation.

Living spaces are on the main level and bedrooms on the upper level. The interior features steeply pitched, wood-beamed cathedral ceilings, oak and green slate floors, and granite countertops. Low eave lines on the upper floor provide for cozy interior spaces with walk-out dormer windows. Forest-green mullioned windows and French doors with access to outdoor decks allow dappled light inside. Handcrafted details include hammered wrought-iron railings, custom-made wood doors, ceramic-tile fireplace fronts, and interior stained glass windows.

The tallest building on the Omaha skyline is the forty-six-story First National Tower. (Leo A Daly)

Entering the New Millennium

The 2000s

Approaching the turn of the millennium and beyond 2000, Nebraska entered a truly remarkable building boom in which "size," "quality," "innovation," and "unconventional" were among the watchwords of the projects. This was found in a new city/regional museum in the western town of Alliance, but particularly seen in Nebraska's largest city.

New development in downtown Omaha was in large part associated with the city's "back to the river" efforts on the Missouri Riverfront. After the removal of the Union Pacific workshops, a lead refinery, and a scrap metal business, the site's building boom included the city's new CenturyLink Center arena/convention center, the Bob Kerry Pedestrian Bridge crossing the river, TD Ameritrade baseball stadium, headquarters operations for the National Park Service and the Gallup Organization, and a new city park.

Even greater impact came to the city skyline due to Omaha's corporate giants. In addition to a major data processing center, First National Bank built its new headquarters building with a forty-six-story skyscraper surpassing the Woodmen Tower as Omaha's tallest. Union Pacific built a dominating new headquarters building, and the *Omaha World-Herald* built a new printing plant. Corporate and individual support provided for a beautiful new performing arts center downtown, and to the south of the business district, an amazing new Desert Dome rose over the Omaha zoo.

The precast concrete walls of the Knight Museum reflect the geology of the Sand Hills.

Knight Museum and Sandhills Center • Alliance

This innovative, historical museum completed in 2008 features five areas of local history including "Life in the Sandhills," "Native American Life," "Life in the Country," "Life in the Town," and "The Railroad That Tied it All Together." The Sand Hills of Nebraska is a vast native grassland sheltering nearly three billion acre-feet of groundwater (the Ogallala Aquifer), and it covers nearly 20,000 square miles in northern and northwestern Nebraska. The essence of the Sand Hills and the life that exists within it becomes a central theme of the structure, created by RDG Planning & Design.

Located within a city park, the original structure was refinished in vernacular materials, and a new roof connects the addition to the old museum. The geology of the Sand Hills is depicted in the precast concrete walls with exposed local aggregates. The large truss on the northeast corner cantilevers seventy-two feet and mimics the idea of a natural sand blowout. The atrium is filled with natural daylight, washing cast-in-place concrete walls with a texture meant to evoke that of the original sod homes of the settlers. The addition relates to its surroundings through form and texture to the rolling hills that form the horizon, and to the built environment that has served and shaped the lives of the Sand Hills dwellers through the centuries.

Prairie Club Lodge • Valentine

Built to take advantage of views of the Nebraska Sand Hills and Snake River Canyon, the lodge at the Prairie Club is a modern landmark that feels part of the surrounding landscape.

The exterior expression of the building is that it is built of natural materials, designed to blend into the high prairie. The building itself is designed to be simple and prairie-like with its wood siding and shingles, with large overhangs for shadows and shade while respecting the natural contours of the land. A great wraparound porch provides a welcoming entry to the building, but also a spectacular view of the Sand Hills, the wooded canyon of the Snake River, and of the Nebraska skies at night.

The Prairie Club Lodge includes 40,000 square feet with twenty-six guest rooms, a restaurant and lounge (overlooking the eighteenth hole of the Pines course), a library and conference room, a cigar bar, a golf shop, locker rooms, and a golf cart garage. The building was designed by Architecture Incorporated of Sioux Falls and opened in 2009.

The Prairie Club Lodge was built to take advantage of the views and vistas of the Snake River Canyon. (Architecture Inc.)

The Great Platte River Road Archway Monument at Kearney was designed to represent a covered bridge crossing Interstate 80.

The Great Platte River Road Archway Monument • Kearney

Few landmark buildings are constructed and moved, but this monument to the pioneer past of Nebraska is anything but conventional.

The first and only museum to straddle an interstate highway was originally conceived by former Nebraska governor Frank Morrison. He desired a major tourist attraction to tell the history of the Platte River trails, from the tribes and the trappers to the wagon trains, stagecoaches, Pony Express, telegraph, railroads, and eventually the highways. The concept evolved to the audacity of building an attraction over the last trail, today's Interstate 80.

The project successfully raised $60 million for the construction of the monument, designed by the Urban Design Group of Denver. The firm designed the structure of exposed weathered steel trusses to represent a covered bridge and to evoke the muscular, bold, and rustic feel of the frontier. The stainless steel exterior was specifically treated with electricity-charged acid to recreate a Nebraska sunset with red, orange, and yellow hues.

The monument was constructed to the side of the interstate while two towers were built to either side of the highway. When complete, the structure was elevated, rolled across the road overnight, and then moved into final position with hydraulic jacks over the next eight days. The attraction was opened to the public in 2000.

The Archway has appeared in the film *About Schmidt* and was the only stop made by President Bill Clinton on his one visit to Nebraska during his term in office.

Designed by the DLR Group, Lincoln's Haymarket Park is a two-time winner of the Baseball Field of the Year Award.

Haymarket Park • Lincoln

The home of the Lincoln Saltdogs and the Nebraska Cornhuskers baseball teams draws its name from the adjacent historic Haymarket warehouse district, which once included scales for the weighing and sale of hay in the capital city's earliest days. Old warehouses are today's restaurants, offices, shops, and residences, with the Haymarket District a highly popular area of the downtown landscape. Tabbing the new park as "Haymarket" immediately places it among the spots for action in Lincoln.

Designed by the DLR Group and opened in 2001 at nearly $30 million, Haymarket Park immediately drew acclaim as one of the best fields in the teams' respective leagues. Hawks Field was the first collegiate ballpark to use a system which can heat and cool the field year-round. For the Saltdogs, it's been selected as the "Best Playing Field" in its league since 2001, and has twice won the Baseball Field of the Year Award in the College/University Division by the Sports Turf Managers Association. In 2012, a college baseball writer ranked the field as the fourth-best big-game atmosphere in Division I baseball.

Total capacity of the park is around 8,500, with seating for 4,500 and the balance on grass berms along the first and third base lines and the outfield areas. The configuration gives the attendees a certain intimacy with the game not found in many parks.

In addition to ball games, Haymarket Park has hosted concerts by the likes of Bob Dylan, Def Leppard, John Mellencamp, and Willie Nelson.

The John Gottschalk Freedom Center was designed to bring the back-room function of newspaper printing to the front and center. (HDR Architecture)

John Gottschalk Freedom Center • Omaha

The *Omaha World-Herald*'s John Gottschalk Freedom Center is among the world's most advanced—and unusual—newspaper production facilities in the world.

Opened in 2001 and designed by HDR Architecture, the Freedom Center is the home to the *Omaha World-Herald*'s 321,000-square-foot press hall and three massive MAN Roland presses from Germany. Through its Transfer Vehicle System, robotic vehicles are used to deliver newsprint from storage directly to the 1,600-ton presses, capable of printing 75,000 newspapers an hour.

Newspaper printing presses are typically located in suburban green-field areas, with printing as a back-room function with the large machinery hidden behind doors and solid walls. At the Freedom Center, the massive presses are the attraction, on full display behind its downtown, street-front glass wall allowing traffic and pedestrians to see the production. Although comprising four city blocks, the tremendous space required forces the center to go vertical with its five-story presses and storage; newsprint rolls are automatically transferred via a sub-street tunnel from the storage facility.

In addition to its status in the print world, the Freedom Center was one of several catalyst projects for the redevelopment of downtown Omaha, along with the Omaha Convention Center and Arena (today's CenturyLink Center Omaha), the First National Center, and the Gallup University campus.

Holy Family Shrine • Gretna

Travelers on Interstate 80 between Omaha and Lincoln are almost certainly surprised by the large, airy building standing tall over the Platte River valley. In the agricultural setting, it almost seems as if it should be a barn or corn crib among the open hills, but study brings the ready impression that this is something spiritual.

Designed by BCDM Architects in Omaha, the Holy Family Shrine was imagined by four anonymous Catholics as a place for the traveler to rest, reflect, and develop and discover their faith in a secluded site without distractions.

The Holy Family Shrine provides a respite for interstate travelers to rest and reflect.

Visitors approach the shrine through a prairie setting, first passing through a tomb-like room embedded in the landscape. A metal sculpture fountain symbolizing the shroud of Christ drips water into a pool and a stream which dissects a stone path leading up and into the chapel.

The chapel is forty-five feet at its tallest point, with its upper trusses interweaving like waves of wheat. The shrine evokes the work of Frank Lloyd Wright apprentice E. Fay Jones, most strongly his Thorncrown Chapel in Eureka Springs, Arkansas. The doors open to the glass-walled chapel, surrounding the indoor space with nature, from the valley below to the sky above.

Ground for the Holy Family Shrine was broken in 1997, but its first rendition was destroyed in a 2000 windstorm. The design was modified to withstand winds and completed in 2002.

First National Tower • Omaha

Omaha's tallest and most visible building, the forty-six-story First National Tower, is equally amazing for what isn't seen.

Beneath the street surface are the building's supports: twenty-eight ninety-inch-diameter shafts, drilled by the world's largest drilling rig and socketed into bedrock. Each shaft is approximately sixty-three feet deep and contains one hundred cubic yards of concrete. After the excavation came Nebraska's largest continuous concrete pour, taking eleven hours to fill the 120-by-76-by-12.5-foot-deep pile cap.

Constructed for the First National Bank of Omaha and designed by Leo A Daly with completion in 2002, the tower is based and piered with granite of a tone reflecting the patterns and colors of the Missouri River. Part of the ground-floor structure is the sixty-foot, glass-enclosed Wintergarden, which incorporates a four-story portion of the 1924 Medical Arts Building that once occupied the space. The indoor space includes a portion of fifty flying, sculpted Canada geese, a portion of a five-block sculpture garden commissioned by First National to celebrate the pioneer spirit and the wilderness faced by the early settlers of Nebraska.

When the concrete core was completed, crews installed the last of the structural steel and the building's exterior skin, including hundreds of unitized aluminum, glass, and Italian granite panels. The tower avoids an over-use of glass as it rises to an eventual pinnacle of 634 feet.

The First National Tower is considered a catalyst for continued public/private investment in the city's downtown revitalization.

The tallest building on the Omaha skyline is the forty-six-story First National Tower.

Within the Desert Dome at Henry Doorly Zoo are a sand waterfall, mountain, canyons, and a cactus forest. (Henry Doorly Zoo & Aquarium)

Desert Dome • Omaha

From the moment the project was announced, the Henry Doorly Zoo's Desert Dome was destined to be THE landmark at the world-famous zoo.

Commanding the quick glimpses of passersby on nearby Interstate 80, the dome is not only the world's largest glazed geodesic dome, but it also houses the world's largest indoor desert. Under its thirteen-story shell, the dome hosts the environments of deserts from Africa, Australia, and the southwestern United States, incorporating nearly fifty desert animal exhibits. Additional features of the $16.5-million structure are a sand waterfall, a fifty-foot mountain, canyons, and a cactus forest. Under the desert floor is a second level, "Kingdoms of the Night," which is the world's largest indoor nocturnal exhibit.

Designed by Stanley J. How and Associates, construction of the dome began in 1999 and was completed in 2002. The Desert Dome consists of 1,760 quarter-inch-thick acrylic, triangular panels of three different shades to provide maximum shade in the summer and maximum light in the winter. Rain falling on the dome is collected in a gutter system and funneled into 20,000-gallon underground storage tanks to be used for watering the plants inside.

The dome contains more than 500,000 pounds of steel reinforcement and holds more than ten thousand tons of concrete in the ringwall and structural slab—the equivalent of a four-inch concrete slab over six and a half football fields. More than two thousand feet of masonry walls enclose animal exhibits, keeper rooms, and holding areas, while another 60,000 masonry blocks form the exhibit rockwork's main support.

CenturyLink Center is Omaha's new riverfront home for major sporting and entertainment events. (Tom Kessler Photography)

CenturyLink Center • Omaha

A small, aged Omaha Civic Auditorium coupled with a desire to bring activity to the downtown riverfront led to the largest public works project in the history of Nebraska.

The 860,000-square-foot CenturyLink Center (originally called the Qwest Center) was one of the first contiguous convention center/arenas in the country, a configuration which has since sent other mid-sized markets to build their own. Since its opening in 2003, the massive structure, owned by the City of Omaha and managed by the Metropolitan Entertainment and Convention Authority, has hosted the Rolling Stones, U2, and other major performing acts, the annual Berkshire-Hathaway meeting with Warren Buffett, NCAA national and regional championships, US Olympic team swimming trials, rodeos and circuses, and hundreds of other events.

With a large exhibition hall, ballroom, meeting rooms, and additional spaces, the CenturyLink Center hosts conferences, expositions, basketball games, and concerts. It is the home court for Creighton University Blue Jays basketball.

DLR Group of Omaha was the design architect for the project, and has since added several expansions and renovations to the facility as the venue has grown in popularity. Upgrades have come to concessions, locker rooms, concourses, and the hospitality club with new consumer demands and sponsorship agreements.

CenturyLink Center has been a driving force for additional development in that part of downtown, particularly with new and expansive lodging and dining opportunities. With its relative nearness to Omaha's Eppley Airfield, it has also become part of the city's welcoming gateway to the downtown area.

The Union Pacific Center provides a dramatic addition to Omaha's headquarters profile, consolidating four thousand employees in one location.

Union Pacific Center • Omaha

In consolidating four thousand employees from ten Omaha locations and its St. Louis office, the Union Pacific Company made the decision to abandon its downtown headquarters building in Omaha and construct an entirely new building across the street.

Opened in 2004 after a two-year build, the Union Pacific Center's 1.3 million-square-foot corporate headquarters features a contemporary glass exterior rising nineteen stories above a stone base. The massive scale of the exterior has been modulated using various glazing technologies and assemblies, which break down the scale of the façades into proportions compatible with nearby structures, while a dramatic full-height central atrium floods the interior with natural light. The design architect for the project was Gensler with Kendall/Heaton Associates as the architect.

The headquarters building also includes a six-hundred-seat cafeteria, fitness center, conference and learning center, data center, broadcasting facilities, and retail spaces.

Omaha's back-to-the-river effort was capitalized with the Carl T. Curtis National Park System Midwest Regional Headquarters and nearby Bob Kerrey Pedestrian Bridge.

Carl T. Curtis NPS Midwest Regional Headquarters • Omaha

This building for the National Park Service (NPS) merged multiple locations into a main office and regional headquarters, and at the same time created a high-tech structure that was environmentally and visitor friendly.

Its location between Omaha's Missouri Riverfront and its downtown—in addition to its highly visible placement near the spectacular Bob Kerrey Pedestrian Bridge—required it to be visually impressive as well. Leo A Daly and Associates designed the headquarters to respond to the city's "back to the river" concept, combining the sweep and contour of the river with the straight-line buildings of the downtown.

The 2004 headquarters project was to support the thirteen states in the NPS's Midwest Region and serve as a permanent museum for Lewis and Clark artifacts relating the history of the river and its importance to the area. The NPS also wanted to make a statement of fiscal responsibility, and the 68,000-square-foot building is the first in Nebraska to qualify for LEED Gold Certification for sustainable design. Through the use of daylight harvesting techniques and integrated sensors to measure daylight and adjust artificial light accordingly, lights turn off automatically in unoccupied rooms. The east-west positioning of the building both reduces heat gain and gives the vast majority of employees a view of the Missouri River.

Priority parking is set aside for carpoolers, with power outlets available for alternative-fuel automobiles. Native plants requiring little or no water surround the building and add to newly created adjacent wetlands.

Holland Performing Arts Center • Omaha

The revitalization of the downtown Omaha core continued in 2005 with the opening of the Holland Performing Arts Center, named in recognition of a gift from Omahans Richard and Mary Holland.

Creation of the Holland Performing Arts Center provided a new home for the musical arts in downtown Omaha. (HDR Architecture)

Positioned along the Gene Leahy Mall, the center provides a highly visible embrace of the musical arts in the city.

The design of the new performing arts center was completed by HDR Architecture in collaboration with Polshek Partnership Architects, joined by acoustic consultants Kirkegaard Associates and theater consultants Fisher Dachs Associates.

The building is clad in zinc, copper, and glass with elevation above the street level. The Holland itself provides a series of spaces for both teaching and performance, including a two-thousand-seat major concert hall, a 450-seat flexible chamber music hall, and an outdoor performance venue within the center courtyard.

Natural light fills the concert hall via a glass clerestory during the day while providing a welcoming beacon at night. The main concert hall is a contemporary interpretation of a shoebox hall, while its narrow shape provides clarity and intimacy to the sound, accentuating the fullness and richness of reverberation. A series of portable platforms allows various types of presentations, and its acoustic conditions can be modified for different performance types.

5550 McKinley House • Omaha

This single-family home began as a 1950s ranch house on ten wooded acres, purchased in 1999 by architect Randy Brown and his wife Kim. They moved into the house and began a phased-construction project in which the home would never truly be completed.

The first phase of construction included a restoration of the surrounding landscape and the establishment of play areas for their two children. The second phase added a three-thousand-square-foot living area onto the existing house, connected by a skywalk. Brown's intention for the home was to explore ways to intertwine the man-made with the natural world, with the house acting as a laboratory.

Toward that goal, the land was sculpted into various forms with man-made geometries. Natural materials like marble and old barn wood are blended with rusted steel and glass. A mowed strip of grass in the shape of a folded line connects the entire project. Portions of the original home were stripped of materials and surfaces, while floor-to-ceiling windows went up in other spaces.

Brown, who also taught architecture at the University of Nebraska at Lincoln and at Omaha, brought in students for the eight-year project to incorporate their skills and share his experience with them.

The Browns have since sold the home, substantially completed but with the hope that it would never be finished.

5550 McKinley is a heavily modified ranch; it was modified to blend the man-made world into the natural world.

TD Ameritrade Park Omaha provides a venue for Creighton University baseball and outdoor sporting and concert events in addition to hosting the NCAA College World Series. (HDR Architecture)

Designing for the Next 150

The 2010s

The construction boom of the preceding decade abated somewhat in the 2010s, but there were still major structures changing the urban landscape of Nebraska's major cities.

Remarkably, many of the larger building projects were focused on Nebraskans' love of sports. The ninety-year-old face of Memorial Stadium at the University of Nebraska at Lincoln was changed forever with the expansion and refacing of the football stadium's entrance. Nearby, a new home for Nebraska basketball and volleyball in Lincoln as well as an exciting new concert venue was finished with the Pinnacle Bank Arena. In Omaha, a new downtown home for the annual College World Series and Creighton baseball was built with TD Ameritrade Park, and a home for University of Nebraska–Omaha hockey was finished with the new Baxter Arena in west Omaha.

The University of Nebraska Medical Center's status as a major medical research and treatment center was cemented with the opening of the new Fred and Pamela Buffett Cancer Center, and a new hospital in Bellevue was designed to blend with the prairie landscape. Energy efficiency and living in harmony with the environment was also a major component of the new SAC Federal Credit Union corporate headquarters building at Papillion.

Nebraska's cultural environment saw longer steps in these years as well, from the new UNL Gaughan Multicultural Center in Lincoln and Blue Barn Theatre in Omaha to the dominating Homestead National Monument Heritage Center in Beatrice and Marjorie K. Daugherty Conservatory at Omaha's Lauritzen Gardens. The state and nation's military preparedness was enhanced with the new Atlas Readiness Center near Mead.

Construction of the Jackie D. Gaughan Multicultural Center was to enhance cultural diversity at the University of Nebraska at Lincoln. (University of Nebraska)

Jackie D. Gaughan Multicultural Center • Lincoln

Constructed in 2010, the Jackie D. Gaughan Multicultural Center is intended as a "home away from home" for minority students at the University of Nebraska at Lincoln while also expanding their role in the larger community.

The center was built adjacent and connected to the Nebraska Student Union, and at 30,000 square feet is the largest such center attached to a student union. In the design from the DLR Group, the façade creates a visual connection between the interior and exterior of the center. The building retains the predominant Colonial design of the campus but adds contemporary ribbons of window wall to "flow" into the student union. The effect is to welcome students into the building, while a grand spiral staircase unites the three levels of open spaces to encourage connection and interaction.

The Gaughan Multicultural Center was a stated priority of the UNL chancellor toward securing and expanding the progress made by UNL in its on-campus diversity efforts. It increases student exposure to services and programs that specifically enhance the understanding and appreciation of cultural diversity. In addition to study, lounge, and conference space, the building hosts a music room, kitchen, and computer lab.

TD Ameritrade Park Omaha • Omaha

Faced with an aging Rosenblatt Stadium and its lack of fan-friendly amenities, as well as a desire to keep the NCAA's College World Series in town, the City of Omaha in 2009 embarked on its first sports-exclusive venue since the late 1940s.

The stadium was designed by HDR Architecture, Populous, and DLR Group and opened by the city in 2011 (with operations by the Metropolitan Entertainment and Convention Authority). The new TD Ameritrade Park Omaha led to the NCAA signing an unprecedented contract to keep the College World Series in the city until at least 2035.

The new 24,000-seat stadium was designed and built to maximize fan convenience. Grand plaza entrances are at each corner of the downtown site. Luxury suites, a 2,400-club-seat lounge, an open concourse, a "Fanfest Area" for activities and games, and a retail zone with views into the bullpen and field were all implemented to bring in the modern fan. Team clubhouse facilities, a central kitchen and commissary, and a press box complete the stadium.

TD Ameritrade Park Omaha provides a venue for Creighton University baseball and outdoor sporting and concert events in addition to hosting the NCAA College World Series. (HDR Architecture)

Besides hosting the annual College World Series, TD Ameritrade Park Omaha is also the home field of the Creighton University Blue Jays and has hosted concerts, football, and hockey events in the infield. Now in its seventh year of operation, the ballpark is established as an icon in college baseball.

Bellevue Medical Center • Bellevue

In designing the Bellevue Medical Center (now Nebraska Medicine–Bellevue), HDR Architecture was tasked with bringing the medical center as close as possible to blending with its surrounding landscape of a mid-grass prairie rather than a bold, contemporary approach.

For example, native grass was used to seed the entire site, and tree species selected were either native or adaptive to the region. The fifty-five-bed, 265,000-square-foot hospital rests lightly on a twenty-two-acre plain without impact to the surrounding native wetlands.

The Prairie style engaged and popularized by Frank Lloyd Wright naturally draws upon the horizontal aspect of the plains, and the hospital was organized into linear wings to tie it into the surrounding plains and highway. A two-story glass entrance transitions movement from the outdoors to the inside; common materials such as grasses, woods, and metals travel from the exterior to the building's interior as well, creating a seamless progression from the prairie to the building exterior to the interior environment.

Simple, linear forms of stone, wood, metal, and glass continue to tie the building to the landscape throughout the floors of the building and into the waiting rooms and the patient rooms. Each uses a color palette featuring muted blues and greens, warm gold and chocolate brown wood tones, and ivory linens.

The carpet, too, holds patterns abstracted from nature, and glass along patient room corridors is etched with a grass motif. The intended result for the hospital opened in 2010 is a warm and welcoming center for patients, creating an environment of a community that nurtures and heals.

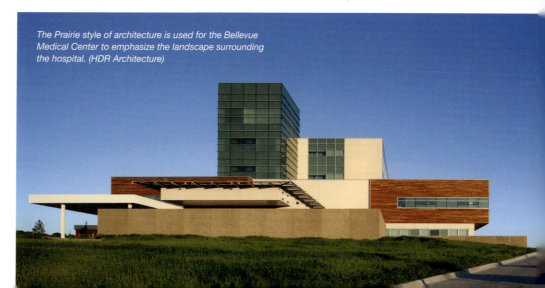

The Prairie style of architecture is used for the Bellevue Medical Center to emphasize the landscape surrounding the hospital. (HDR Architecture)

Numerous expansions to the University of Nebraska's Memorial Stadium have changed the face of the nearly century-old sporting venue.

Memorial Stadium • Lincoln

It was Roscoe Pound who first encouraged the game of football at the University of Nebraska in 1890, having witnessed the enthusiasm for the 1889 Harvard/Yale game while a law student at Harvard. The Nebraska native knew the game would catch on, and Chancellor Canfield saw it as an opportunity to build public goodwill for the school. A team was organized and games were played on an open field with grandstands, regularly filling with fans for the sport. The "Cornhuskers'" defeats of legendary teams like Notre Dame's Knute Rockne and the Four Horsemen brought calls for a larger facility—perhaps a stadium to handle more ticket sales.

That move took place in 1923 with the construction of the first rendition of Memorial Stadium, built to honor the memory of soldiers killed in the recent World War and previous wars. Underwritten by the Nebraska Alumni Association through donations, original plans were for a $1 million project including a football stadium, a gymnasium, a World War I museum, and a veterans' club; those plans were drastically scaled back when a legislative appropriation was cut.

The association hired two architects for the stadium: Latenser & Sons of Omaha and Davis & Wilson in Lincoln. Both firms donated their services, saving the association $25,000 in costs. Construction of the field and the east and west stadiums was completed in less than ninety days—in time for the first game of the 1923 season.

Memorial Stadium's original capacity was slightly more than 31,000; the only other addition in the next forty years was the Field House at the north end zone in the 1940s. With the addition of a winning coach in Bob Devaney, four expansions were made in the 1960s to more than double the seating and turn the stadium into a bowl configuration. Expansions and additions continued through the 1990s with a new press box, skyboxes, club seating, and bleacher seating.

The last major addition to Memorial Stadium came in 2013 with the East Stadium expansion, designed by the Clark Enersen Partners. The expansion increased seating to more than 90,000 and created a dramatic new entrance for the stadium while preserving the original East Stadium exterior within its concourse. The new facing of the stadium incorporated pressed red brick for the first time, providing a stronger tie to the surrounding campus buildings using the same building medium.

The Marjorie K. Daugherty Conservatory established the Lauritzen Gardens as a year-round tourism attraction. (HDR Architecture)

Marjorie K. Daugherty Conservatory at Lauritzen Gardens • Omaha

The first structure seen by visitors to Nebraska from westbound Interstate 80 is the spectacular Marjorie K. Daugherty Conservatory and adjacent visitor center at Lauritzen Gardens. The 17,500-square-foot glass palace appears to emerge from Missouri River bluffs onto a plateau rising above the river.

Until its construction in 2014, Omaha's botanical garden wasn't a true year-round attraction. The addition of this "oasis in the city," however, has transformed the Lauritzen into one of Omaha's most popular destinations.

Designed by HDR Architecture and landscape architect CG Studios, the Daugherty Conservatory takes a Classical approach to conservatories and presents its display as a series of gently cascading gardens, including more than three thousand non-Nebraska plants and flowers. Visitors to the glassed structure do have to make a twenty-foot climb via stairs (or an elevator) to reach its northern entrance and begin a slow, meandering, downward stroll to the southern face of the structure.

The conservatory essentially takes in two climates, beginning with a ten-thousand-square-foot tropical house featuring towering palm trees, exotic flowers, and a ten-foot waterfall, moving into a 5,300-square-foot temperate garden with plants and antebellum architectural features resembling an old Southern garden, and a two-thousand-square-foot gallery for alternating floral displays and special events.

An open, airy, sustainable environment is the emphasis of the SAC Federal Credit Union corporate headquarters building. (Leo A Daly)

SAC Federal Credit Union Corporate Headquarters • Papillion

The SAC Federal Credit Union corporate headquarters building is not your traditional banking building.

The front doors open into the headquarters' four-story communication core atrium, highlighted by a striking "floating" staircase of laminated oak planks and see through railings. Every glass-doored office within the building opens into the atrium, with the intention of the openness to increase collaboration and communication within the organization. The airiness continues with a roof-top patio and fourth-floor balcony.

The four-story, 94,000-square-foot structure, designed by Leo A Daly and opened in 2014, incorporates sustainable materials throughout. Features include radiant heating, water pipes in the ceilings and walls for heating and cooling effects, and reuse of energy normally lost to exhaust. Its lighting includes LED and fluorescent lamps that automatically dim and brighten based on daylight conditions. Utility costs are estimated to drop by 30 percent, largely aided by more than two hundred wells dug three hundred feet deep into the south side of the property connected to heat pumps, moving heat to water when cooling and absorbing heat from water when heating.

Additional high-tech features include a branch office that goes without teller lines and safety deposit box access through digital reading of fingerprints. Ultimately holding 140 employees, the headquarters building hosts a fitness center for corporate fitness incentives and a community meeting room for the credit union's nonprofit and community partners.

Baxter Arena • Omaha

Baxter Arena was built as the cornerstone of a plan to consolidate University of Nebraska–Omaha athletics in one location, but since its opening in 2015, the arena has already proved its attractiveness as a mid-sized, community-wide facility.

Located to the immediate south of the bustling Aksarben Village, the arena is the home of UNO hockey, men's and women's basketball, and volleyball. It has also hosted concerts, civic events, high school graduations, campus recreation, youth hockey, figure skating, and curling. Unusual for a facility of this type, but to emphasize its outreach to the community, the practice ice rink is also a community rink and is the focal point for visitors entering the arena.

The impetus for Baxter Arena began in 2012 with the announced closing of the Omaha Civic Auditorium because of maintenance costs of the aging facility. The resulting need for a mid-sized indoor venue and a new home for the popular UNO hockey program put the creation of the arena on the fast track. Working from a design by HDR Architecture, the structure was funded and built through a joint community/university partnership and completed in eighteen months. The building (which is owned by UNO) seats just under eight thousand with seventeen luxury suites and additional standing-room space.

Baxter Arena makes an unusual emphasis on the public community rink at its main entrance. (HDR Architecture)

Homestead National Monument Heritage Center • Beatrice

Dedicated in 2007, the Heritage Center at Homestead National Monument provides a new interactive environment for explorers of a landmark piece of American legislation.

The Homestead Act of 1862 ultimately—over the course of 123 years—led to the settlement of more than 270 million acres in thirty states by about 1.6 million people. Among the first of those land claims was filed by pioneer Daniel Freeman, who filed his claim within minutes after the law took effect. His 160-acre homestead is now the site of the National Park Service's national monument and the spectacular Heritage Center.

The exterior of the 10,600-square-foot center clearly symbolizes the single-bottom plow, which was used to break the prairie sod, with the roof of the "plow" pointing the way to the American West overlooking the monument site.

The center, designed by GWWO of Baltimore, presents twenty-one exhibit areas to view artifacts and tell the story of the legislative act and its impact on the settlement of the West. Also included are a theater, information services, bookstore, curatorial and office spaces, and a public research area.

The exterior of the Homestead National Monument Heritage Center was designed to symbolize the single-bottom plow, which was used to break the prairie sod.

The Atlas Readiness Center near Mead occupies grounds once hosting Atlas ballistic missiles. (RDG)

Atlas Readiness Center • Mead

Taking its name from the intercontinental ballistic missile silos that once shared its grounds, the Atlas Readiness Center near Mead is dedicated to the future of Nebraska's National Guard.

The $10.8 million facility, opened in 2013 as the home to the 402nd Military Police Battalion, provides a base for the tactical training of guard units with missions in Iraq, Afghanistan, and other areas that may arise. The 48,000-square-foot space includes classroom and physical training space, while the 1,100-acre grounds are spacious enough for tent-scenario immersion training.

Designed by RDG, the center has a LEED Silver sustainability rating. The design uses wood beams and decking as used in National Guard facilities of the past, while providing a modern facility with today's technologies. A portion of the interiors are exposed precast concrete, which include an acid-etch finish. The highlight of the precast portion of this project is the interior corridor exposing a repeating pattern of a customized pixilated form liner on buff-colored precast wall panels.

Blue Barn Theatre • Omaha

Well established as Omaha's professional theatre after twenty-five years in the city, the Blue Barn Theatre sought a new home that reflected its heritage of innovation and risk-taking.

Omaha architects Min | Day designed the new home (opened in 2015) from the ground up with the theatre as its core. From the stage, a large custom door opens the backstage to a semi-enclosed outdoor performance area, which in turn connects to the "Green in the City" open space. This pioneering arrangement supports a multitude of theatre configurations, from the usual proscenium to the less-typical alley theatre and environmental theatre forms.

The intention of the project, said architect Jeff Day, was to maintain the Blue Barn's "intimacy and its funky, eclectic feel." His firm sought a collective and collaborative approach to this urban environment with the expectation that the facility will continue to evolve.

The Blue Barn Theatre uses a variety of building materials to create intimacy and a "funky, eclectic feel."

The Pinnacle Bank Arena's multistory glass-fronted lobby gives passersby a view of inside activity. (DLR Group)

Pinnacle Bank Arena • Lincoln

Built as the centerpiece of the $340 million Haymarket District development, the Pinnacle Bank Arena provides a top-tier venue for sports and entertainment events in the capital city.

Completed in 2013, the 470,000-square-foot arena replaced the Bob Devaney Sports Center as the home of University of Nebraska men's and women's basketball games. In addition to providing an intense atmosphere (16,000 seats) for university sports and high school state tournaments, it is also the Lincoln site of the top touring musical acts in the country. The Eagles, Elton John, Paul McCartney, and Bruno Mars are among the many making stops at "The Vault."

The arena was designed by the DLR Group with a multistory glass-fronted lobby that gives passersby a view of activity on all levels of the building, but also gives patrons a view of the Haymarket, downtown Lincoln, and the Nebraska State Capitol. Besides the general seating, the lower seating bowl features nine hundred club seats and a dedicated club lounge located immediately behind them on the main concourse, along with twelve-person suites and twenty-four-person loge boxes on the premium level. The split upper deck allows concourse patrons a view to the event floor below, and also allows the top seating bowl to pull closer to the floor for an intimidating wall of fans surrounding the event.

Fred and Pamela Buffett Cancer Center • Omaha

The potential for advances in cancer research and treatment led the University of Nebraska board of regents to move toward a massive coordination of all cancer research activities within the Fred and Pamela Buffett Cancer Center at the UNMC campus in Omaha.

Named for its major donors (the late Fred Buffett was a first cousin of noted Omaha investor Warren Buffett), the cancer center is a fully integrated environment bringing patients, clinicians, and researchers closer, to speed treatment from laboratory to bedside.

Designed by HDR Architecture, the $323 million, 615,000-square-foot center (opened in 2017) is the largest project in the university's history and the largest public/private partnership in the history of Nebraska. Funding included $50 million from the state, $35 million from the City of Omaha, $5 million from Douglas County, and the balance from private contributions. It will draw patients from western Iowa, eastern South Dakota, northeastern Kansas, and northwestern Missouri, in addition to Nebraska.

The L-shaped building is composed of two towers: the Suzanne and Walter Scott Research Tower, housing the ten-story, ninety-eight-lab cancer research facility, and the eight-story, 108-bed C. L. Werner Cancer Hospital inpatient treatment center. For the patients' respite and reflection, the center also includes the spectacular Chihuly Sanctuary art installation as part of its healing arts program.

The Fred and Pamela Buffett Cancer Center at the University of Nebraska Medical Center is the largest public/private partnership in the history of Nebraska. (HDR Architecture)

Bibliography

BOOKS

Drenna, Lynne, et. al. *Omaha City Architecture.* Omaha: Landmarks Inc. and Junior League of Omaha, 1977.
Gerber, Kristine and Jeffrey S. Spencer. *Building for the Ages: Omaha's Architectural Landmarks.* Omaha: Landmarks Inc., 2003.
Gibbs, Dale L. Foreword to *An Architectural Album.* Lincoln: Junior League of Lincoln, 1979.
Hall, Loretta. *Underground Buildings: More Than Meets the Eye.* Sanger, CA: Quill Driver Books, 2004.
Hendee, David. *Nebraska: 150 Years Told Through 93 Counties.* Marceline, MO: Walsworth Publishing, 2016.
Luebke, Frederick C., ed. *A Harmony of the Arts: The Nebraska State Capitol.* Lincoln and London: University of Nebraska Press, 1990.
Luebke, Frederick C. *Nebraska: An Illustrated History.* 2nd ed. Lincoln and London: University of Nebraska Press, 2005.
McKee, James L. *Lincoln: A Photographic History.* Lincoln: Salt Valley Press, 1976.
Mills, Nicolaus. *Their Last Battle: The Fight for the National World War II Memorial.* (Memorial Park in Omaha) New York: Basic Books, 2004, pp. XXIII–XXIV.
Olson, James C. and Ronald C. Naugle. *History of Nebraska.* 3rd ed. Lincoln and London: University of Nebraska Press, 1997.
Ripley, Robert C. Foreword to *The Nebraska State Capitol: Restoring a Landmark.* Omaha: Omaha Books, 2013.
Wishart, David J., ed. *Encyclopedia of the Great Plains.* Lincoln and London: University of Nebraska Press, 2004.
Wrightsman, B. "Re-Envisioning the Knot: The Neil Astle House." In *Structures and Architecture: Beyond Their Limits*, edited by Paulo J. S. Cruz. Boca Raton, FL: CRC Press, 2016.

NATIONAL REGISTER OF HISTORIC PLACES NOMINATION FORMS

Adams, Diana K. *Kearney United States Post Office,* National Register of Historic Places Inventory/Nomination Form, US Postal Service, Field Real Estate & Buildings Office, Mission, KS, January 30, 1981.
Adams, George R. *Arbor Lodge,* National Register of Historic Places Inventory/Nomination Form, American Association for State and Local History, Nashville, TN, September 1, 1974.
Ahlgren, Carol. *Plainview Band Shell,* National Register of Historic Places Inventory/Nomination Form, Nebraska State Historical Society, Lincoln, July 1, 1992.
Arbogast, David, et al. *Freeman Homestead and Freeman School,* National Register of Historic Places Inventory/Nomination Form, National Park Service, Omaha, December 19, 1975.
Callahan, Bill. *Fairmont Army Airfield,* National Register of Historic Places Inventory/Nomination Form, Nebraska State Historical Society, Lincoln, October 22, 2002.
Chase, Elizabeth. *Bassett Lodge and Range Café,* National Register of Historic Places Inventory/Nomination Form, Nebraska Lied Main Street, Lincoln, April 2006.
Chatfield, Penelope. *Anheuser-Busch Office Building,* National Register of Historic Places Inventory/Nomination Form, Nebraska State Historical Society, Lincoln, December 1, 1978.
———. *Scout's Rest Ranch,* National Register of Historic Places Inventory/Nomination Form, Nebraska State Historical Society, Lincoln, July 1977.
———. *Father Flanagan's House,* National Register of Historic Places Inventory/Nomination Form, Nebraska State Historical Society, Lincoln, July 1979.
———. *Hotel Flatiron,* National Register of Historic Places Inventory/Nomination Form, Nebraska State Historical Society, Lincoln, July 1, 1978.
———. *US Indian School,* National Register of Historic Places Inventory/Nomination Form, Nebraska State Historical Society, Lincoln, March 1977.
Dirr, Melissa A. *Weber Mill,* National Register of Historic Places Inventory/Nomination Form, Nebraska State Historical Society, Lincoln, September 3, 1998.
Dolberg, Jill E. *Nebraska Governor's Mansion,* National Register of Historic Places Inventory/Nomination Form, Nebraska State Historical Society, Lincoln, November 30, 2007.
———. *Broomfield Rowhouse,* National Register of Historic Places Inventory/Nomination Form, Nebraska State Historical Society, Lincoln, December 12, 2006.
Ebeling, Mary R., et al. *Karl Stefan Memorial Airport Administration Building,* National Register of Historic Places Inventory/Nomination Form, Mead & Hunt, Inc., Madison, WI, July 2001.
Ebers, Jill M. *Walter Behlen House,* National Register of Historic Places Inventory/Nomination Form, Nebraska State Historical Society, Lincoln, October 29, 2002.
———. *Wayne Municipal Auditorium,* National Register of Historic Places Inventory/Nomination Form, Nebraska State Historical Society, Lincoln, November 30, 2001.
———. *West Lawn Mausoleum,* National Register of Historic Places Inventory/Nomination Form, Nebraska State Historical Society, Lincoln, July 13, 2004.
Edwards, Rae, et al. *Dr. Susan Picotte Memorial Hospital,* National Register of Historic Places Inventory/Nomination Form, Center for Rural Affairs, Walthill, August 1, 1988.
Ehlers, D. Layne. *Love-Larson Opera House,* National Register of Historic Places Inventory/Nomination Form, Nebraska State Historical Society, Lincoln, April 1, 1988.
———. *ZCBJ Opera House,* National Register of Historic Places Inventory/Nomination Form, Nebraska State Historical Society, Lincoln, May 16, 1988.
Fagler, James T. *Cathedral of the Nativity of the Blessed Virgin Mary,* National Register of Historic Places Inventory/Nomination Form, Nebraska Historical Society, Lincoln, June 1982.
———. *St. John's German Evangelical Lutheran Church,* National Register of Historic Places Inventory/Nomination Form, Nebraska State Historical Society, Lincoln, May 13, 1982.
Gamble, Robert S. *Willa Cather House,* National Register of Historic Places Inventory/Nomination Form, National Park Service, Washington, DC, July 19, 1971.

Gengler, Melissa Dirr, et al. *Sheldon Memorial Art Gallery*, National Register of Historic Places Inventory/Nomination Form, Nebraska State Historical Society, Lincoln, April 2013.

Gilkerson, Joni. *Oak Ballroom*, National Register of Historic Places Inventory/Nomination Form, Nebraska State Historical Society, Lincoln, September 1, 1982.

———. *St. Bonaventure Catholic Church Complex*, National Register of Historic Places Inventory/Nomination Form, Nebraska State Historical Society, Lincoln, August 1982.

Gilkerson, Joni, et al. *Temple of Congregation B'Nai Jeshuran*, National Register of Historic Places Inventory/Nomination Form, Nebraska State Historical Society, Lincoln, March 1982.

Gorgen, Barbara A. *Wright Morris Boyhood Home*, National Register of Historic Places Inventory/Nomination Form, Lone Tree Literary Society, Central City, August 1980.

Hajek, Timothy J. *Champion Mill*, National Register of Historic Places Inventory/Nomination Form, Champion Mill State Historical Park, Champion, February 24, 1988.

Hughes, Patricia A. *Evans House*, National Register of Historic Places Inventory/Nomination Form, (N/A), November 12, 1990.

Hurst, Robert. *Lincoln Army Air Field Regimental Chapel*, National Register of Historic Places Inventory/Nomination Form, (N/A), Lincoln, March 1993.

———. *Midwest Theater*, National Register of Historic Places Inventory/Nomination Form, Panhandle Landmarks Inc., Lincoln, April 1, 1997.

Ireland, Lynne. *Fort Hartsuff Historic District*, National Register of Historic Places Inventory/Nomination Form, Nebraska Game and Parks Commission, Lincoln, January 15, 1977.

Jeffries, Janet. *Glur's Tavern*, National Register of Historic Places Inventory/Nomination Form, Nebraska State Historical Society, Lincoln, May 16, 1975.

———. *McCormick Hall*, National Register of Historic Places Inventory/Nomination Form, Nebraska State Historical Society, Lincoln, January 30, 1975.

———. *Nye House*, National Register of Historic Places Inventory/Nomination Form, Nebraska State Historical Society, Lincoln, November 1, 1976.

———. *Otoe County Courthouse*, National Register of Historic Places Inventory/Nomination Form, Nebraska State Historical Society, Lincoln, October, 1975.

———. *Patterson Law Office*, National Register of Historic Places Inventory/Nomination Form, Nebraska State Historical Society, Lincoln, January, 1979.

———. *The Elms-Bess Streeter Aldrich Home*, National Register of Historic Places Inventory/Nomination Form, Nebraska State Historical Society, Lincoln, April 14, 1976.

Jorgensen Unick, Lori. *Barnes Oil Company*, National Register of Historic Places Inventory/Nomination Form, Jorgensen Unick Design, Lincoln, August 2002.

Kidd, Daniel. *Omaha (Central) High School*, National Register of Historic Places Inventory/Nomination Form, Nebraska State Historical Society, Lincoln, August 1, 1979.

———. *St. Cecilia Cathedral*, National Register of Historic Places Inventory/Nomination Form, Nebraska State Historical Society, Lincoln, November 1, 1978.

Kolberg, Persijs. *Astro Theatre*, National Register of Historic Places Inventory/Nomination Form, Nebraska State Historical Society, Lincoln, (N/A).

———. *Old Log Cabin*, National Register of Historic Places Inventory/Nomination Form, Nebraska State Historical Society, Lincoln, September 27, 1970.

———. *The Mansion on the Hill*, National Register of Historic Places Inventory/Nomination Form, Nebraska State Historical Society, Lincoln, (N/A).

———. *Fort Sidney Historic District*, National Register of Historic Places Inventory/Nomination Form, Nebraska State Historical Society, Lincoln, (N/A).

———. *Frank House*, National Register of Historic Places Inventory/Nomination Form, Nebraska State Historical Society, Lincoln, November 30, 1972.

———. *Jefferson County Courthouse*, National Register of Historic Places Inventory/Nomination Form, Nebraska State Historical Society, Lincoln, April 11, 1972.

———. *Joslyn Castle*, National Register of Historic Places Inventory/Nomination Form, Nebraska State Historical Society, Lincoln, (N/A).

———. *US Post Office and Courthouse*, National Register of Historic Places Inventory/Nomination Form, Nebraska State Historical Society, Lincoln, April 24, 1974.

———. *Omaha Building*, National Register of Historic Places Inventory/Nomination Form, Nebraska State Historical Society, Lincoln, February 14, 1978.

———. *Rock Island Depot*, National Register of Historic Places Inventory/Nomination Form, Nebraska State Historical Society, Lincoln, May 17, 1971.

———. *Starke Round Barn*, National Register of Historic Places Inventory/Nomination Form, Nebraska State Historical Society, Lincoln, October 12, 1971.

———. *Trinity Episcopal Church*, National Register of Historic Places Inventory/Nomination Form, Nebraska State Historical Society, Lincoln.

———. *Union Station–Durham Museum*, National Register of Historic Places Inventory/Nomination Form, Nebraska State Historical Society, Lincoln, September 22, 1971.

———. *US Post Office–Courthouse (Nebraska City)*, National Register of Historic Places Inventory/Nomination Form, Nebraska State Historical Society, Lincoln, May 27, 1971.

Lissandrello, Stephen. *Fort Robinson and Red Cloud Agency*, National Register of Historic Places Inventory/Nomination Form, National Park Service, Washington, DC, September 27, 1976.

———. *William Jennings Bryan Home*, National Register of Historic Places Inventory/Nomination Form, National Park Service, Washington, DC, July 1, 1975.

———. *Senator George W. Norris House*, National Register of Historic Places Inventory/Nomination Form, National Park Service, Washington, DC, July 29, 1975.

Long, Barbara Beving. *Cass County Courthouse*, National Register of Historic Places Inventory/Nomination Form, Four Mile Research Co., Des Moines, IA, November 8, 1989.

———. *Hooker County Courthouse*, National Register of Historic Places Inventory/Nomination Form, Four Mile Research Co., Des Moines, IA, November 12, 1989.

———. *Johnson County Courthouse*, National Register of Historic Places Inventory/Nomination Form, Four Mile Research Co., Des Moines, IA, November 8, 1989.

———. *Lincoln County Courthouse*, National Register of Historic Places Inventory/Nomination Form, Four Mile Research Co., Des Moines, IA, November 12, 1989.

———. *Sherman County Courthouse,* National Register of Historic Places Inventory/Nomination Form, Four Mile Research Co., Des Moines, IA, November 8, 1989.

Long, Christine and Emily Pettis. *Northern Natural Gas Building*, National Register of Historic Places Inventory/Nomination Form, Mead & Hunt, Inc., Madison, WI, March 1, 2009.

Magie, John Q. *Bank of Florence*, National Register of Historic Places Inventory/Nomination Form, Nebraska State Historical Society, Lincoln, August 22, 1969.

———. *First Presbyterian Church*, National Register of Historic Places Inventory/Nomination Form, Nebraska State Historical Society, Lincoln, July 10, 1970.

———. *General Crook House*, National Register of Historic Places Inventory/Nomination Form, Nebraska State Historical Society, Lincoln, February 21, 1969.

———. *Brownville Historic District*, National Register of Historic Places Inventory/Nomination Form, Nebraska State Historical Society, Lincoln, March 31, 1970.

———. *John G. Neihardt Study*, National Register of Historic Places Inventory/Nomination Form, Nebraska State Historical Society, Lincoln, (N/A).

———. *Nebraska Statehood Memorial*, National Register of Historic Places Inventory/Nomination Form, Nebraska State Historical Society, Lincoln, February 21, 1969.

———. *Neligh Mill*, National Register of Historic Places Inventory/Nomination Form, Nebraska State Historical Society, Lincoln, August 27, 1969.

———. *Phelps Hotel*, National Register of Historic Places Inventory/Nomination Form, Nebraska State Historical Society, Lincoln, July 9, 1970.

———. *US Post Office and Courthouse*, National Register of Historic Places Inventory/Nomination Form, Nebraska State Historical Society, Lincoln, August 22, 1969.

Meyer, Lynn, et al. *Livestock Exchange Building*, National Register of Historic Places Inventory/Nomination Form, Omaha City Planning Department and Nebraska State Historical Society, March 1, 1999.

Miller, Greg. *GAR Memorial Hall*, National Register of Historic Places Inventory/Nomination Form, Nebraska State Historical Society, Lincoln, November 1993.

———. *Linoma Beach Lighthouse*, National Register of Historic Places Inventory/Nomination Form, Nebraska State Historical Society, Lincoln, August 2002.

———. *Norden Bombsight Vault*, National Register of Historic Places Inventory/Nomination Form, Nebraska State Historical Society, Lincoln, January 1993.

———, et al. *Argo Hotel*, National Register of Historic Places Inventory/Nomination Form, Nebraska State Historical Society, Lincoln, December 1998.

———. *Burlington Station*, National Register of Historic Places Inventory/Nomination Form, Nebraska State Historical Society, Lincoln, August 1977.

———. *Elijah Filley Stone Barn*, National Register of Historic Places Inventory/Nomination Form, Nebraska State Historical Society, Lincoln, April 1976.

———. *Hall County Courthouse*, National Register of Historic Places Inventory/Nomination Form, Nebraska State Historical Society, Lincoln, November 24, 1976.

———. *Omaha Public Library*, National Register of Historic Places Inventory/Nomination Form, Nebraska State Historical Society, Lincoln, February 1978.

———. *Sutton House*, National Register of Historic Places Inventory/Nomination Form, Nebraska State Historical Society, Lincoln, January 1978.

———. *William R. Dowse House*, National Register of Historic Places Inventory/Nomination Form, Nebraska State Historical Society, Lincoln, April 1986.

———, et al. *States Ballroom*, National Register of Historic Places Inventory/Nomination Form, Nebraska State Historical Society, Lincoln, August 1981.

Peters, Robert, *St. John's AME Church.* National Register of Historic Places Inventory/Nomination Form, Omaha City Planning Department, April 1, 1980.

———, et al. *Jewell Building*, National Register of Historic Places Inventory/Nomination Form, Nebraska State Historical Society, Lincoln, July 9, 1970.

Pitts, Carolyn. *Nebraska State Capitol*, National Register of Historic Places Inventory/Nomination Form, National Park Service, Washington, DC, July 1975.

Spencer, Janet Jeffries, et al. *Chautauqua Pavilion*, National Register of Historic Places Inventory/Nomination Form, Nebraska State Historical Society, Lincoln, April 1978.

———. *Hotel Wilber*, National Register of Historic Places Inventory/Nomination Form, Nebraska State Historical Society, Lincoln, July 1978.

———. *Pilgrim Holiness Church*, National Register of Historic Places Inventory/Nomination Form, Nebraska State Historical Society, Lincoln, May 1979.

Stupka-Burda, Stacy, et al. *Nebraska State Historical Society Building*, National Register of Historic Places Inventory/Nomination Form, Nebraska State Historical Society, Lincoln, April 14, 2003.

Zimmer, Edward F. *Municipal Lighting and Waterworks Plant*, National Register of Historic Places Inventory/Nomination Form, Lincoln/Lancaster County Planning Department, Lincoln, April 25, 1986.

NEWSPAPERS AND PERIODICALS

"As Much a Piece of Art . . ." (NBC Center in Lincoln), *Lincoln Evening Journal*, May 2, 1976.

"Historic Places: The National Register for Nebraska," *Nebraska History*, Vol. 70, No. 1, Spring 1989.

INTERNET

"About Benedictine Retreat Center—Christ the King Priory." https://christthekingpriory.com/ckpabout/.

"About the Archway," The Archway–Kearney, Nebraska. http://archway.org/about-the-archway/.

"About the Center for Biotechnology," (Information on the Beadle Center). https://biotech.unl.edu/about-center.

"About Us," Strategic Air Command & Aerospace Museum. https://sacmuseum.org/about-us/.

"Architecture," First-Plymouth Congregational Church. http://www.firstplymouth.org/architecture/.

"Atlas Readiness Center," RDG Planning & Design. https://www.rdgusa.com/projects/atlas-readiness-center.

"Bell tower plays modern music for all to enjoy," (Feature on Peterson-Yanney Carillon Tower), UNK Communications, February 12, 2014. http://unknews.unk.edu/2014/02/12/bell-tower-plays-modern-music-for-all-to-enjoy/.

"Bellevue Medical Center / HDR Architecture," *Arch Daily*, March 21, 2011. http://www.archdaily.com/110399/bellevue-medical-center-hdr-architecture.

"Benedictine Mission House." http://www.reinhardtarchitects.com/reinhardt_project_religious_benedictinemission.htm.

"Blue Barn Theater & Boxcar 10," October 2015. http://www.minday.com/Blue-Barn-Theater-Boxcar-10.

"Cancer Center Blends Research & Clinical Services to Accelerate Discovery," HDR Architecture. https://www.hdrinc.com/portfolio/fred-pamela-buffett-cancer-center.

Carl T. Curtis Midwest Regional Headquarters of the National Park Service, Omaha, NE. https://www.gsa.gov/real-estate/design-construction/design-excellence/sustainability/sustainable-design/leed-building-information/leed-case-studies/carl-t-curtis-midwest-regional-headquarters-of-the-national-park-service-omaha-ne.

"CenturyLink Center Omaha Convention Center and Arena," DLR Group. http://www.dlrgroup.com/work/centurylink-center-omaha-convention-center-and-arena/.

Daly, Leo A. "First National Tower." http://www.leoadaly.com/portfolio/first-national-tower/.

"Danish Brotherhood Building Passes First Landmark Test," Restoration Exchange Omaha, April 8, 2016. http://www.restorationexchange.org/2016/04/08/danish-brotherhood-building-passes-first-landmark-test/.

Davis, Joan. "A History of the Grand Island Public Library, 1884–1984," City of Grand Island. (Website) http://www.grand-island.com/your-government/library/about-your-library/library-history/library-history-by-joan-davis.

Deck, Emily. "Group incorporates to save farmhouse linked to Otoe tribe," (Otoe-Missouria Mission School) *Beatrice Daily Sun*, September 15, 2013. http://beatricedailysun.com/news/local/group-incorporates-to-save-farmhouse-linked-to-otoe-tribe/article_f74eb8c4-4ebd-57db-b8fa-6ab96405849f.html.

"Desert Dome and Kingdoms of the Night—Henry Doorly Zoo," ASD Stanley J. How Architects. http://www.asdhow.com/zoo/44-articles/zoo/34-desert-dome-and-kingdoms-of-the-night-henry-doorly-zoo.

"Gene Leahy Mall—Landscape Information." https://tclf.org/landscapes/gene-leahy-mall.

"Hawks Field at Haymarket Park," NU Athletic Communications. http://www.huskers.com/ViewArticle.dbml?ATCLID=717.

"History of Memorial Stadium," NU Athletics Communication. http://www.huskers.com/ViewArticle.dbml?ATCLID=1097233.

"Holy Family Shrine." http://www.holyfamilyshrineproject.com/.

"Homestead Heritage Center," National Park Service. https://www.nps.gov/home/heritagecenter.htm.

"Homestead Heritage Center," Archinect. https://archinect.com/firms/project/15387532/homestead-heritage-center/147738605.

"Jackie D. Gaughan Multi-Cultural Center," DLR Group. http://www.dlrgroup.com/work/jackie-d-gaughan-multicultural-center/.

"John Gottschalk Freedom Center," *Omaha World-Herald*. http://www.owh.com/who-we-are/the-john-gottschalk-freedom-center/.

Kaarre, Jourdyn. "Woodmen Tower, dedicated in, 1969, aided the rebirth of downtown Omaha," *Omaha World-Herald*, June 6, 2014. http://www.omaha.com/money/woodmen-tower-dedicated-in-aided-the-rebirth-of-downtown-omaha/article_d49ae496-f312-50b7-86ce-4eee4791ecbb.html.

Knight Museum. http://knightmuseum.com/.

"Lauritzen Gardens' $20M conservatory another 'amazing icon' for Omaha," *Omaha World-Herald*, October 8, 2014. http://www.omaha.com/news/metro/kelly-lauritzen-gardens-m-conservatory-another-amazing-icon-for-omaha/article_9d6d2160-4ead-11e4-96e8-001a4bcf6878.html.

Milton R. Abrahams Branch, Omaha Public Library. https://omahalibrary.org/about-abrahams/.

"Nebraska National Guardsmen put training to the test at new center near Mead, Neb.," (Feature on Atlas Readiness Center), *Omaha World-Herald*, September 12, 2013. http://www.omaha.com/news/nebraska-national-guardsmen-put-training-to-the-test-at-new/article_85989deb-84c4-55c2-8040-ee2097faca1a.html.

"Nebraska's Largest Art Museum," Joslyn Art Museum. https://www.joslyn.org/about/history/.

"Omaha architect transforms woodland house into 'laboratory,'" (Feature on 5550 McKinley Home), *Omaha World-Herald*, July 8, 2013. http://www.omaha.com/living/omaha-architect-transforms-woodland-house-into-laboratory/article_cd21ed5e-c6dc-55f8-b430-bf5e79834ee4.html.

"Our Commitment to the Future," Lied Conference Center. https://www.liedlodge.org/about/environmental-commitment.cfm.

"Pinnacle Bank Arena," DLR Group. http://www.dlrgroup.com/work/pinnacle-bank-arena/.

"SAC Opens New Corporate Headquarters," SAC Federal Credit Union. http://www.sacfcu.com/sac-opens-new-corporate-headquarters.php.

"St. Columbkille Parish History." http://saintcolumbkille.org/wordpress/index.php/about-us/parish-history/.

"Stations between Fort Kearney and Horseshoe Creek," (Information on Midway Station at Gothenburg), Pony Express Historic Resource Study, National Park Service. https://www.nps.gov/parkhistory/online_books/poex/hrs/hrs5a.htm.

"Strauss Performing Arts Center," College of Communication, Fine Arts and Media. https://www.unomaha.edu/college-of-communication-fine-arts-and-media/music/about-us/spac.php.

"Stuhr Museum of the Prairie Pioneer, Classic Buildings—Society of Architectural Historians," Archipedia. http://sah-archipedia.org/buildings/NE-01-079-0051.

"TD Ameritrade Park Omaha: Fostering Civic Pride and Community Connectivity," HDR Architecture. https://www.hdrinc.com/portfolio/td-ameritrade-park-omaha.

"The Prairie Club Golf Lodge," Architecture Incorporated. http://www.architectureinc.com/work/prairie-club-lodge/.

Union Pacific Center. http://www.kendall-heaton.com/projects/union-pacific-center/.

"UNL Historic Buildings—Behlen Laboratory of Physics." http://historicbuildings.unl.edu/building.php?b=98.

"UNL Historic Buildings—Memorial Stadium." http://historicbuildings.unl.edu/building.php?b=38.

"UNL Historic Buildings–Mueller Tower." http://historicbuildings.unl.edu/building.php?b=91.

"UNL Historic Buildings—Old Library" (Reference on Architecture Hall, University of Nebraska–Lincoln campus). http://historicbuildings.unl.edu/building.php?b=12.

"UNO's rising arena, finances both solid," (Feature on Baxter Arena), *Omaha World-Herald*, October 6, 2014. http://www.omaha.com/news/metro/uno-s-rising-arena-finances-both-solid/article_c1e9bd99-ae9c-51cc-872e-281c53255a87.html.

"Why the Holland Resonates on Multiple Levels," HDR Architecture. https://www.hdrinc.com/portfolio/holland-performing-arts-center.

"Wick Alumni Center," Nebraska Alumni Association. http://www.huskeralum.org/s/1620/social.aspx?sid=1620&gid=1&pgid=434.

"With five academic units spread across campus, CFAM students live and learn in a wide variety of educational environments," UNO CFAM. https://www.unomaha.edu/college-of-communication-fine-arts-and-media/about-us/facilities.php.

Acknowledgments

Putting this book together was one of the most joyful experiences in my life, and I have a number of people to thank for helping me find that joy and hopefully sharing in it.

First of all, my thanks to Bruce Carpenter, president of the Architectural Foundation of Nebraska, and to Sara Kay, director of the American Institute of Architects–Nebraska Chapter. I've known both of these fine individuals for many years and worked with them on several projects. The opportunity to tell the story of the state we love through its buildings was a unique and wonderful challenge that they offered, and their confidence and support through the process of creating this book will always have my appreciation. My thanks to Nate Ehmke, also in the AIA–Nebraska office, for his constant efforts in keeping us on track and working together.

Bob Ripley, capitol administrator of the Nebraska State Capitol, and Matt Hansen, preservation architect of the capitol, were of great assistance and particularly in aspects of the career of Thomas Rogers Kimball. We have all been great fans of Nebraska's greatest architect, but their professional insights and advice were invaluable. I've known Bob since my association with the Nebraska Hall of Fame in the early 1990s, and it was more than a pleasure to be able to work with him again.

Marty Shukert, former city planner for the City of Omaha, also was a helpful adviser, especially in highlighting the work and impact of the late Neil Astle. Nebraska has a rich architectural history, and Marty helped me gain an appreciation of this innovative master.

Randa Zalman of Canary & Coal loaned her marketing agency's research capability, and her intern Kyleigh Smart tracked down information on the more current projects featured in the book. Thank you, Kyleigh, and thank you, Randa, for your ever-faithful friendship and advice.

This is my third book with Barry Haire of Donning Company Publishers and our best book to date. Barry is always a great partner, with both first-time publishers and those who have done a few. He's become a good friend over the years, and I think Bruce and Sara will say they valued the time of working with him as well. I also want to thank my editor Heather Floyd at Donning; she provided excellent editing and follow-up advice, and mostly kept me on track in completing coverage of 150 sites. Likewise to Terry Epps at Donning for his great work in building the book and my heartfelt appreciation to Tom Kessler, Sarita Hollander, Craig Chandler, and Andrea Terryberry for their last-minute photo assistance.

My thanks to Mom and Dad—it's because of them that I was born, raised, and will always be Nebraskan. They gave me an appreciation of the history and heritage of the state and continue to support my work.

Finally, my gratitude and love to my wonderful wife Susan for seeing me through another book. This one is a bit more special in that it was through this book's most spectacular building that we met, she as a capitol tour guide and I as an unpaid student reporter for a Sand Hills radio station. She's the one who suffers under the inevitable rants and interruptions to family time when I'm doing these, but she also shares in the excitement when they're done. Patience is a virtue and a blessing, and I am blessed to have her with me.

Jeff Barnes
Omaha, Nebraska
October 8, 2017

Index

"A" Street Power and Water Station, 75
5550 McKinley House, 139

A

Aldrich, Bess Streeter, 77
Alexander, Hartley Burr, 86, 88
Alley Poyner Macchietto Architecture, 33, 124
Alliance (Neb.), 130
American Institute of Architects, 61, 117
Anheuser-Busch Office Building, 33
Arbor Lodge, 53
Architecture Hall, 47
Architecture Incorporated (architects), 130
Argo Hotel, 64
Arthur (Neb.), 81
Arthur County Historical Society, 81
Architectural styles
    Art Deco, 85, 86, 87, 88, 90, 93, 99, 102
    Beaux-Arts, 13, 34, 51, 55, 75, 86
    Chateauesque, 36, 38, 42
    Classic Revival, 51
    Classical, 34, 55, 61, 80, 88, 109, 145
    Colonial Revival, 64, 95
    English Tudor, 90
    French Renaissance Revival, 65
    French Second Empire, 26, 32
    Georgian Revival, 23, 66, 76, 81, 104
    Gothic Revival, 17, 52
    Greek Revival, 11, 12, 19, 64, 69
    High Victorian Gothic, 15, 26
    Italian Renaissance, 33, 43, 82
    Italianate, 13, 17, 23, 24, 25, 30, 32, 53
    Late Gothic Revival, 31, 73, 83
    Medieval Scotch Baronial, 52
    Modern Movement, 101, 102, 103, 107
    Modernism, 88, 109, 113
    Moorish, 78, 80
    Neo-Classical, 49, 71, 75, 88
    Neo-Colonial, 53
    Postmodern/Late National Romantic, 110
    Prairie, 58, 64, 74, 77, 143
    Property-type, 36, 75
    Queen Anne, 51
    Renaissance, 64, 121
    Richardsonian Romanesque, 37, 39, 44
    Roadside Architecture, 89
    Romanesque Revival, 32, 33, 36, 40, 70, 82
    Second Renaissance Revival, 43, 54
    Spanish Colonial Revival/Spanish Renaissance, 51, 56, 61, 64
    Streamline Moderne, 96
Ashland (Neb.), 75, 89, 126
Astle, Neil (architect), 107, 109, 110, 111, 112, 113
Astle/Ericson & Associates (architects), 110, 116
Astro Theater, 80
Atlas Readiness Center, 149

B

Bacon, Henry (architect), 68
Bahr, Vermeer & Haecker (architects), 108, 120, 122
Bancroft (Neb.), 46
Bank of Florence, 11
Barnes Oil Company, 89
Barnes, Francis and Mary Jane, 22
Barneston (Neb.), 22
Bassett (Neb.), 102
Bassett Lodge and Range Café, 102
Baxter Arena, 147
BCDM Architects, 133
Beadle Center for Genetics, 125
Beadle, George W., 125
Beatrice (Neb.), 16, 19, 148
Bee (Neb.), 94
Behlen (Walter and Ruby) House, 105
Behlen Laboratory of Physics, 109
Behlen, Walter and Ruby, 105
Bell, W. E. (architect), 36
Bellevue, 9, 10, 12, 143
Bellevue Medical Center/Nebraska Medicine–Bellevue, 143
Berggren Architects, 89
Berlinghof, George A. (architect), 78
Big Springs (Neb.), 31
Bloor, Elle Reeve "Mother", 75
Blue Barn Theatre, 150
Bob Kerrey Pedestrian Bridge, 137
Bowen House, 127
Bowen, Gary (architect), 127
Boys Town, 81, 98
Brandhoefer Mansion, 33
Brandhoefer, Leonidas A., 33
Brcin, John David, 86
Brinkman, Henry W. (architect), 83
Broomfield Rowhouse, 67
Broomfield, John H. "Jack", 67
Brown, Randy (architect), 139
Brownville (Neb.), 16
Bryan, William Jennings, 49, 50, 57
Bucher, William and Joseph, 24
Buffett Cancer Center, 151
Buffett, Fred and Pamela, 151
Burlington Railroad, 15, 46, 49, 51, 60, 63
Burwell (Neb.), 21
BVH Architecture, 108, 120

C

Carl T. Curtis NPS Midwest Regional Headquarters, 138
Carnegie, Andrew, 63
Cass County Courthouse, 40
Cathedral of the Nativity of the Blessed Virgin Mary, 83
Cather, Willa, 27
Central City (Neb.), 19, 42
Central Park Mall/Gene Leahy Mall, 113, 114
CenturyLink Center, 133, 136
Champion (Neb.), 41
Champion Mill, 41
Chautauqua, 49, 57
Chautauqua Pavilion, 57
Cheyenne County Museum, 18
Chicago and Northwestern Railroad, 64

Christensen, Emiel (architect), 91
Clark Enerson (architectural firm), 42, 145
Clarkson (Neb.), 69
Clinton, Bill, 131
Cody House, 32
Cody, William F. "Buffalo Bill", 24, 32
Columbus (Neb.), 24, 64, 105, 109
Crawford (Neb.), 24
Crazy Horse, 24
Crofton (Neb.), 64
Crook, Gen. George A., 25
Cunningham, Harry F. (architect), 88, 104
Czechs in Nebraska, 29, 45, 50, 68, 94

D

Daly, Leo A. (architect), 98
Daly, Leo A., Jr. (architect), 111
Danish Brotherhood Building, 107, 110
Danish Brotherhood in America, 110
Davis & Wilson (architects), 78, 99, 103, 144
Davis Design (architects), 124
Davis, Ellery (architect), 78, 103
Davis, Fenton, Stange & Darling (architects), 115
Day, Jeff (architect), 150
Desert Dome, 135
Devaney, Bob, 145
DLR Group (architects), 132, 136, 142, 150
Douglas County Historical Society, 25
Dowse House, 50
Dreamland Ballroom, 74, 77
Dufrene, Alfred (architect), 31

E

Eberson, John (architect), 80
Edith Abbott Memorial Library, 117
Elarth, Hershel (architect), 61, 86
Elijah Filley Stone Barn, 20
Ellis, Francis M. (architect), 34
Evans House, 64
Evans, Dr. Carroll and Lorena, 64

F

Fairbury (Neb.), 40, 63
Fairmont (Neb.), 95
Fairmont Army Airfield, 95
Fairview, 50
Father Flanagan's Home, 81
Filley (Neb.), 20
Filley, Elijah, 20
First National Tower, 111, 128, 129
First Presbyterian Church (Bellevue), 12
First United Methodist Church, 100, 104
First-Plymouth Congregational Church, 87
Fisher & Lawrie (architectural firm), 44, 47
Fiske & Meginnis (architects), 75
Florence (Neb.), 10, 11
Fort Hartsuff State Historical Park, 21
Fort Omaha, 25
Fort Robinson, 24
Fort Robinson Adobe Officers' Quarters, 24
Fort Sidney, 18
Frank House, 37
Frank, George William, 37
Frank, George William, Jr. (architect), 37
Freed, James Ingo (architect), 115
Freeman School, 19
Freeman, Daniel, 19, 148
Fremont (Neb.), 23, 34
French, Daniel Chester, 68

G

Galleher, Tom (architect), 102
GAR Memorial Hall, 44
General Crook House, 25
Genoa (Neb.), 59
Gensler (architects), 136
Germans in Nebraska, 29, 50, 52, 63, 70, 94, 116
Glur, Louis, 24
Glur's Tavern, 24
Goodhue, Bertram Grosvenor, 61, 88
Goodman, Julia (Cody), 32
Gothenburg (Neb.), 12
Gov. Robert W. Furnas House, 16
Grabe, George (architect), 90
Grand Army of the Republic, 39, 44
Grand Island (Neb.), 55, 66, 73, 83, 108, 117
Grant, Ulysses S., 25
Gray, William (architect), 36, 40
Great Platte River Road Archway, 131
Gretna (Neb.), 133
Guth, J. P. (architect), 52
Gwathmey/Siegel & Associates (architects), 121
GWWO (architects), 148

H

Hagan, J. Stanley (architect), 83
Hall County Courthouse, 55, 60
Hall County Historical Society, 108
Harrison, Henry G. (architect), 31
Hastings (Neb.), 30, 49, 51, 57
Hastings Burlington Station, 51
Hastings College, 30
Haymarket Park, 132
HDR Architecture, 75, 86, 133, 138, 143, 145, 147, 151
Henninger, Frederick A. (architect), 76
Henningson Engineering Company, 75
Henry Doorly Zoo, 135
Holland Performing Arts Center, 138
Holland, J. C. (architect), 40
Holland, Richard and Mary, 138
Holy Family Shrine, 133
Homestead Act, 15, 44, 68, 148
Homestead National Monument, 16, 19, 148
Homestead National Monument Heritage Center, 148
Hooker County Courthouse, 66
Hotel Flatiron, 66
Hotel Wilber, 45
Hunt, Jarvis (architect), 53

I

I. M. Pei and Partners (architects), 115

J

Jack D. Wilkins & Associates (architects), 122
Jackie D. Gaughan Multicultural Center, 142
Jefferson County Courthouse, 39
Jewell Building, 73, 76
Jewell, James C., Sr., 76
John G. Neihardt Study, 46
John Gottschalk Freedom Center, 133
Johnson County Courthouse, 36
Johnson, Philip (architect), 108
Jones, E. Fay (architect), 134
Joslyn Castle, 52
Joslyn Memorial Museum (Joslyn Art Museum), 86
Joslyn, George and Sarah, 52, 86

K

Karl Stefan Memorial Airport Administration Building, 96

Kearney (Neb.), 37, 71, 118, 122, 131
Keith County Historical Society, 33
Kendall/Heaton Associates (architects), 136
Kennard, Thomas Lord, 61
Kimball, Thomas Rogers, 39, 43, 48, 49, 51, 53, 55, 56, 60–61, 63, 66, 67, 68, 70, 82, 86, 87, 88, 109
Kinkaid Act, 49, 66
Kinkaid, Moses P., 49
Kirschke, Oscar R. (architect), 66
Knight Museum and Sandhills Center, 130
Kountz, Augustus F., 66
Kuska, George (architect), 99

L

Lackaff, Floyd and Maude, 102
LaFlesche, Joseph, 68
Larson, L. P., 34
Latenser & Sons (architects), 102, 144
Latenser, Frank (architect), 104
Latenser, John (architect), 65
Lauritzen Gardens, 145
Lawrence Halprin & Associates (architects), 114
Lawrie, Lee, 88
Leo A Daly and Associates (architects), 105, 120, 126, 128, 134, 138, 146
Lied Center for the Performing Arts, 123
Lied Lodge and Conference Center, 124
Liederkranz, 66
Lincoln (Neb.), 14, 15, 17, 26, 38, 39, 42, 47, 50, 75, 78, 87, 88, 95, 99, 103, 104, 108, 109, 115, 121, 123, 124, 132, 142, 144, 149
Lincoln Army Airfield, 95
Lincoln Army Airfield Regimental Chapel, 95
Lincoln County Courthouse, 78
Lincoln Memorial, 68
Linoma Beach Lighthouse, 89
Livestock Exchange Building, 82
Log Cabin (Bellevue), 8, 10
Louis E. May Trust, 23
Loup City (Neb.), 75
Love, James Wheeler, 34
Love-Larson Opera House, 34
Lyons (Neb.), 52

M

Magonigle, Harold Van Buren (architect), 87
Marjorie K. Daugherty Conservatory, 145
Massachusetts Institute of Technology, 60
McCook (Neb.), 46, 58, 96
McCook Army Air Base, 96
McCormick Hall, 30
McCormick, Cyrus H., 30
McDonald, John (architect), 52, 86
McKim, Mead and White (architects), 34, 43
McLaughlin, Robert W., Jr. (architect), 87
McMill Building, 54
Mead (Neb.), 149
Meginnis & Schaumberg (architects), 99
Meiere, Hildreth, 88
Memorial Stadium, 141, 144
Mendelssohn, Fisher & Lawrie (architects), 47
Meridian Highway, 64
Metropolitan Community College, 25
Metropolitan Entertainment and Convention Authority, 135, 142
Midway Station, 12
Midwest Theater, 92, 97
Milton R. Abrahams Public Library, 120
Min | Day (architects), 150
Mormons, 9, 10
Morton, J. Sterling, 49, 53

Mueller Tower, 99
Mueller, Ralph, 99
Mullen (Neb.), 66
Mullet, Alfred (architect), 26
Museum of Nebraska Art, 71
Mutual of Omaha Dome, 120

N

Nachtigall, Jacob (architect), 61, 62, 70, 81
National Park Service, 16, 19, 129, 137, 148
National Register of Historic Places, 7, 34, 55, 69, 78, 89, 108
NBC Center/Wells Fargo Center, 115
Nebraska Alumni Association, 121
Nebraska City (Neb.), 9, 13, 28, 36, 44, 53, 124
Nebraska Game and Parks, 32, 41, 53
Nebraska Governor's Mansion, 104
Nebraska State Architects' Association, 104
Nebraska State Capitol, 61, 68, 73, 85, 88, 101, 103
Nebraska State Historical Society, 17, 20, 27, 46, 51, 101, 103, 121
Nebraska State Historical Society Foundation, 17
Neihardt, John G., 46
Neligh (Neb.), 20
Neligh Mill, 20
Neligh, John D., 20
Norden Bombsight Vault, 96
Norfolk (Neb.), 54, 94, 96
North Platte (Neb.), 29, 32, 78
Northern Natural Gas Building, 101, 102
Nye House, 23
Nye, Theron, 23

O

Oak Ballroom, 90
Ogallala (Neb.), 33
Omaha (Neb.), 9, 11, 15, 25, 29, 31, 32, 34, 41, 43, 52, 56, 60–61, 65, 66, 67, 68, 74, 76, 80, 81, 86, 98, 101, 102, 110, 111, 114, 120, 125, 127, 129, 133, 135, 136, 137, 138, 139, 142, 145, 147, 150, 151
Omaha Building, 34, 35
Omaha Central High School, 135
Omaha Indian Reservation, 68
Omaha Indians, 12
Omaha Public Library, 43, 60
Oregon Trail, 12
Oregon Trail Community Foundation, 97
Ostenberg, William H., Jr., 97
Otoe County Courthouse, 13
Otoe Indians, 12, 22
Otoe-Missouria Mission School, 22

P

Palmer-Epard Cabin, 16
Papillion (Neb.), 122, 146
Patterson Law Office, 19
Peter Kiewit and Sons Construction Company, 82
Peterson, George and Venetia, 122
Peterson-Yanney Bell Tower, 118, 122
Phelps Hotel, 31
Phelps, Edwin A., 31
Picotte Memorial Hospital, 68
Picotte, Dr. Susan LaFlesche, 68
Pilgrim Holiness Church, 73, 81
Pinnacle Bank Arena, 150
Plainview (Neb.), 94
Plainview Band Shell, 94
Plattsmouth (Neb.), 40
Polshek Partnership Architects, 138
Pony Express, 9, 12, 131
Potter, William Appleton (architect), 26

Prairie Club Lodge, 130
Prinz, George B. (architect), 61, 66, 82
Public Works Administration (PWA), 90, 91

R
Raeville (Neb.), 70
RDG Planning & Design (architects), 130
Red Cloud (Neb.), 27, 55
Roberts, Artemis A. (architect), 50
Rock Island Depot, 39, 42
Roosevelt, Eleanor, 95
Roosevelt, Franklin D., 85
Roosevelt, Theodore, 61, 117

S
SAC Federal Credit Union Corporate Headquarters, 146
Saint-Gaudens, Louis, 34
Sarpy County Historical Society, 10, 12
Sarpy, Peter, 10
Schemmer (architects), 125
Schuyler (Neb.), 91, 116
Scottsbluff (Neb.), 93, 97
Scout's Rest Ranch, 32
Sen. George W. Norris House, 46
Sessinghaus, Edward J. (architect), 104, 110
Sheldon Museum of Art, 108
Sheldon, A. Bromley, 108
Sheldon, Frances, 108
Sherman County Courthouse, 75
Sidney (Neb.), 18
Smith, Linus Burr (architect), 99, 104
Sobotka, Vladimir (architect), 94
Sod homes, 49, 50, 81, 130
Solheim, Selmer A. (architect), 104
St. Benedict Center, 113, 116
St. Benedict Monastery, 112, 116
St. Bonaventure Catholic Church, 62, 70
St. Cecilia Cathedral, 48, 49, 55, 56, 61
St. Columbkille Catholic Church, 122
St. John African Methodist Episcopal Church, 73, 74
St. John's German Evangelical Lutheran Church, 52
St. Joseph and Denver City Railroad, 51
St. Mary's Cathedral, 72, 73, 83
Stanford White (architect), 34
Stanley J. How and Associates (architects), 117, 135
Starke Round Barn, 55
States Ballroom, 94
Steele Sandham and Weinstein (architects), 109
Steele, William (architect), 61, 68, 108
Stefan, Karl, 96
Stone, Edward Durell (architect), 107, 108
Stott, Frederick S. (architect), 74
Strategic Air Command Museum, 126
Strauss Performing Arts Center, 114
Strauss, Willis A. and Janet S., 114
Strong, Charles D. (architect), 97
Stuhr Museum of the Prairie Pioneer, 108
Stuhr, Leo, 108
Sutton House, 58
Sutton, Harvey and Eliza, 58

T
Taylor, James Knox (architect), 54, 71
TD Ameritrade Park, 140, 142
Tecumseh (Neb.), 36
Teig & Johnson (architects), 110
Temple of Congregation B'Nai Jeshuran, 73, 78
The Elms, 77
The Rose, 80

Thomas P. Kennard House, 17
Thornburgh, Maj. Thomas T., 31
Trinity Episcopal Cathedral, 31
Truman, Harry S., 98

U
US Army Corps of Engineers, 95
US Indian School, 59
US Post Office and Courthouse (Kearney), 71
US Post Office and Courthouse (Lincoln), 14, 26
US Post Office and Courthouse (Nebraska City), 28, 36
US Post Office and Courthouse (Norfolk), 54
Underwood, Gilbert Stanley (architect), 87
Union Station–Durham Museum, 86
Union Pacific Railroad, 15, 18, 31, 42, 49, 60, 87, 129, 136
Union Pacific Center, 137
University of Nebraska Medical Center, 29, 124, 141, 151
University of Nebraska–Kearney, 37, 122
University of Nebraska–Lincoln, 47, 99, 108, 109, 121, 124, 142, 144
University of Nebraska–Omaha, 114, 125, 147
Unthank, John O. (architect), 89
Urban Design Group (architects), 131

V
Valentine (Neb.), 130
Voss, Henry (architect), 32

W
Wagoner, Harold Eugene (architect), 100, 105
Walker & Kimball (architectural firm), 43, 60
Walker, C. Howard (architect), 60
Watson, Elbert B. (architect), 94
Wayne (Neb.), 90
Wayne Municipal Auditorium, 90
Weber Fine Arts Building, 125
Weber Mill, 10
Weber, Del and Lou Ann, 125
Welk, Lawrence, 91
West Lawn Mausoleum, 68
Wick Alumni Center, 121
Wick, Milton J., 121
Wiggington, Clarence (architect), 61, 67
Wilber (Neb.), 45
Willa Cather House, 27
Winchell, John K. (architect), 17
Winter Quarters, 10
Woodmen Tower, 106, 107, 111, 129
Works Progress Administration (WPA), 91, 93, 94, 96
World War II, 20, 69, 89, 93, 95, 96, 98, 99, 102, 109
World War II Memorial Park, 98
Wounded Knee, 18
Wright Morris Boyhood Home, 42
Wright, Frank Lloyd (architect), 49, 58, 134, 143
Wurdeman, Charles H. (architect), 64

Y
Yanney, Elias and Mary, 122

Z
ZCBJ Opera House, 69
Zenon, Golden (architect), 114